The Soul-Winner's Toolbox
Practical Guide for Effective Evangelism
Useful For Pastors, and Church Leaders in Training

By

Nicole Bennett Blake

Copyright © 2024 by Nicole Bennett Blake. All rights reserved.

"No part of this book may be reproduced, stored in a retrieval system, or transmitted in any form or by any means, whether electronic, mechanical, photocopying, recording, or otherwise, without prior written permission from the publisher."

This book is intended to provide practical guidance for effective evangelism and serves as a valuable resource for pastors and church leaders in training. The techniques, strategies, and insights shared herein are the result of the author's extensive experience and research in evangelism.

While every effort has been made to ensure the accuracy and reliability of the information presented, the author and publisher assume no responsibility for errors, inaccuracies, or omissions. Readers are advised to use their discretion and judgment in applying the principles discussed to their specific contexts.

Any references to individuals, organizations, or events are purely coincidental. The views and opinions expressed in this book are those of the author and do not necessarily reflect the official policy or position of any entity mentioned.

DEDICATION

"To all 'Christian' believers, pastors, and church leaders who have a burning passion for souls and a relentless commitment to sharing the life-changing message of the Gospel:

This book, The Soul Winner's Toolbox: A Practical Guide for Effective Evangelism Useful for Pastors and Church Leaders in Training, is dedicated to you."

1. **Passion for Souls:** Your unwavering desire to see people come to faith in Christ has inspired the creation of this practical resource. It is my hope that the tools and strategies within these pages will empower you to fulfil your calling with renewed zeal and effectiveness.
2. **Personal Experiences:** Your personal encounters with individuals in need of the Gospel have deeply impacted your heart and fueled your desire to equip others for soul-winning. May your experiences continue to serve as a powerful reminder of the urgency and importance of sharing the love of Christ with others.
3. **Gap in Resources:** Recognizing the need for practical resources tailored specifically to pastors and church leaders, this book seeks to fill a gap in existing materials. It is my prayer that the insights and strategies provided herein will address real-world challenges and equip you for greater effectiveness in your evangelistic efforts.
4. **Desire for Discipleship:** Beyond the initial act of evangelism, your desire for discipleship and the nurturing of new believers is evident. May this book not only serve as a tool for winning souls but also as a guide for effectively discipling and nurturing the spiritual growth of those who respond to the Gospel message.
5. **God's Call:** Above all, it is my firm belief that this work is inspired by a divine calling. May you be encouraged and emboldened by the knowledge that God has entrusted you with the mission of impacting lives for eternity through the proclamation of His Word.

May this book serve as a beacon of hope and guidance for all who seek to share the Good News of Jesus Christ with a world in need. May it inspire and equip you to fulfill your God-given mandate with courage, conviction, and compassion.

With deepest gratitude and admiration for your dedication to the Great Commission,

Nicole Bennett Blake

Table of Contents

"The Soul-Winner's Toolbox: A Practical Guide to Effective Evangelism" 1

PART I 3

Chapter One: Introduction: "Doing It Jesus' Way: 4

Chapter Two: How Can I Overcome Fear of Evangelism? 43

PART II: Share Your Story 84

Chapter Three: Unveiling Grace: Sharing Your Personal Testimony 85

Chapter Introduction 85

Chapter Four: Crafting Conversations Beyond Words: 105

Encouragement: 120

Chapter Five: Discipling the Disciple – Unleashing the Soul Winner Within 128

Practical Tips: 142

Chapter Six: Planting Seeds of Faith 150

Testimonials 156

Conclusion 170

Recommended Reading resources 172

Bibliography 173

Acknowledgements 174

About the Author 177

Nicole Bennett Blake

"THE SOUL-WINNER'S TOOLBOX: A PRACTICAL GUIDE TO EFFECTIVE EVANGELISM"

"In a world crying out for hope, the message of Christ stands a the ultimate answer, a beacon of light in the darkness and a promise of eternal peace for all who believe.

As believers, we carry a sacred responsibility to share Christ's life-transforming message with a hurting humanity. This book is more than ink on paper; it's a torch passed from one soul winner to another, illuminating the path to eternity."

Introduction

"For God so loved the world that He gave His only begotten Son, that whoever believes in Him should not perish but have everlasting life." — John 3:16

"The Soul-Winner's Toolbox" is born from the trenches of street corners, hospital rooms, and kitchen tables. Its pages bear the fingerprints of countless encounters: **tear-streaked faces, trembling hands, and hearts on the brink of surrender. The author, a seasoned evangelist, has traversed continents, knocking on doors and whispering hope into the darkest corners** of humanity.

Purpose and Urgency

"The urgency of our times cannot be overstated. The ticking clock of eternity compels us to action. As the shadows lengthen, we must rise—bold, unyielding, and armed with the Gospel. This book provides practical, battle-tested strategies for effective evangelism tailored for pastors, and church leaders in training."

What You'll Discover

1. **Practical Strategies: From street evangelism to house-to-house visits, we** explore **methods that work. Learn how to engage hearts,** address **objections, and lead souls to the** Saviour.

2. **The Heart of Evangelism:** It's not about eloquence or charisma; it's about compassion. Discover the power of a listening ear, a warm smile, and a heart aflame with love.
3. **Pitfalls and Triumphs:** We explore the highs and lows, the moments when souls embrace salvation and the times when rejection stings. Even in setbacks, we find divine appointments.
4. **The Message:** Our Redeemer's story, the cross, the resurrection, the hope, is our message. We equip you to share it with clarity, conviction, and unwavering faith.

Why This Book Matters

"How then shall they call on Him in whom they have not believed? And how shall they believe in Him of whom they have not heard? And how shall they hear without a preacher?" —Romans 10:14

"The **SOUL-WINNER** Toolbox" isn't just ink on paper; it's a lifeline to the lost. It's a plea to the Church: **LET** us not hoard the Good News but scatter it like seeds **UP** on fertile soil. The world awaits its harvest, and **YOU**—the soul **WINNER**—are the **LABOURER** in God's vineyard.

So, dear reader, sharpen your sickle, gird your loins, and step into the fields. The harvest is ripe, and eternity hangs in the balance.

May this book ignite a fire within **YOU**—a passion to win souls, one heart at a time. Let the pages turn, and may your footsteps echo the **SAVIOUR'S** call: "Follow Me, and I will make you fishers of men."

Nicole Bennett Blake

PART I

CHAPTER ONE:
INTRODUCTION: "DOING IT JESUS' WAY:

A Blueprint for Effective Evangelism

"And Jesus came and spoke to them, saying, 'All authority has been given to Me in heaven and on earth. Go therefore and make disciples of all the nations, baptizing them in the name of the Father and of the Son and of the Holy Spirit, teaching them to observe all things that I have commanded you; and lo, I am with you always, even to the end of the age, (Matthew 28:18-20 NKJV)

In this pivotal chapter, we step into the sandals of the Master Evangelist Himself, Jesus Christ. His approach to soul-winning transcends mere technique; it embodies love, compassion, and divine authority. As we explore "Doing It Jesus' Way," we uncover timeless principles that resonate across cultures, generations, and hearts hungry for truth.

1. The Heartbeat of Compassion

"When He saw the multitudes, He was moved with compassion for them, because they were weary and scattered, like sheep having no shepherd. (Matthew 9:36 NKJV)"

Jesus' approach to evangelism was not a mechanical checklist; it flowed from a heart that bled for humanity. He saw beyond external appearances, perceiving the brokenness, the weariness, and the longing, and met people where they were. As we embark on this journey, let us ask: How can we cultivate compassion? How can our eyes mirror His, seeing souls rather than statistics?

2. The Art of Storytelling

Jesus wove truth into stories, the parables. He understood that narratives penetrate deeper than facts. Whether by the seashore or on a mountainside, He painted vivid pictures of grace, redemption, and the Kingdom. As soul winners, can we learn to tell stories that resonate with the human heart, stories that echo eternity, mend bridges, and restore relationships?

"And He spoke many things to them in parables. (Matthew 13:3 KJV)"

The Parable of the Sower in Matthew 13:3-8 serves as a practical guide for soul winners by highlighting the importance of the "soil," or the hearts of people. It teaches that:

1. **Not all will receive the message:** Just as some seeds fell on the path and were eaten by birds, some people will not understand or accept the Word.
2. **Expect challenges:** Seeds that fell on rocky ground sprouted quickly but withered without deep roots, symbolizing those who initially receive the message with joy but fall away when troubles arise.
3. **Distractions can hinder growth:** Seeds among thorns represent people choked by life's worries and wealth, preventing them from maturing spiritually.
4. **Be patient and persistent:** Good soil produced a crop, showing that diligent sowing and nurturing can lead to fruitful outcomes.

For soul winners, this parable emphasizes the importance of preparing hearts to receive the gospel, being patient with growth, and understanding that not every attempt will be successful, but perseverance can lead to rewarding results.

3. **The Power of Presence**

"And Jesus went about all Galilee, teaching in their synagogues, preaching the gospel of the kingdom, and healing all kinds of sickness and all kinds of disease among the people. (Matthew 4:23NKJV)"

Jesus did not only preach from a synagogue; He walked dusty roads, touched lepers, and dined with sinners. His presence carried healing, hope, and transformation. As we engage in evangelism, let us remember that our lives, the way we love, serve, and listen, speak louder than words. How can we be present in a world craving authenticity?

4. The Call to Discipleship

"Follow Me, and I will make you fishers of men. (Matthew 4:19 KJV)"

Jesus did not recruit spectators; He called disciples. He invited fishermen, tax collectors, and zealots into a radical journey of transformation. Evangelism isn't a one-time transaction; it's an invitation to walk alongside the Saviour. How can we lead others to follow Jesus, not just as converts but as committed followers?

5. The Promise of Immanuel

"Behold, the virgin shall be with child, and bear a Son, and they shall call His name Immanuel, which is translated, 'God with us. (Matthew 1:23 NKJV)"

The heartbeat of Jesus' evangelism resonates in this name: Immanuel, God with us. He promised His abiding presence, even as we step into the harvest fields.

"And he said unto them, go ye into all the world, and preach the gospel to every creature. (Mark 16:15 NKJV)"

"As you go into all the world, preach openly the wonderful news of the gospel to the entire human race. (Mark 16:15 TPT)"

Imagine a church where every Christian is comfortable going out into their world and evangelise the way Jesus did. It is good to preach the Gospel of Jesus Christ to large crowds, but the simple truth is that many lost sinners will never hear a sermon unless some Christian brings them to a gospel meeting. They will not respond to the invitation unless a Christian encourages them to go forward and claim Christ. Many would not know how to trust Christ or have the assurance of salvation if a personal worker did not show them from the Scriptures. The way God wants us to bring the message of the gospel is to tell people about His unique Son, Jesus Christ. Every time Jesus preached the gospel, He spoke about the kingdom of God, in which Yahweh is King.

Nicole Bennett Blake

Most people generally think of "preaching the Gospel" as delivering a sermon to a crowd. However, when we examine Scripture, it shows that this is not the principal meaning of the Great Commission. We should read the Great Commission as it is written: "Go ye into all the world and preach the Gospel." The Great Commission does not mention any church buildings, nor does it mention congregations. No, the Lord Jesus is talking about individuals here. We are to preach the Gospel "to every creature," that is, to every individual in our world or circle. Christ did not die for congregations; He died for individuals. The Great Commission is not to preach the Gospel to congregations but to individuals. Your world consists of the people in your community with whom you have day-to-day contact, the people you encounter.

The winning of souls is the responsibility of every believer; it is the most precious thing you will ever experience in your life. All Christians have the obligation to share the Gospel; it should be on the heart of every believer to look for opportunities to share the life of Jesus with a broken world.

The winning of individuals by individuals in personal conversation is the main way to win souls. Having a heart to personally go out and speak with individuals is key to winning souls, and is the method most clearly commanded in the Bible.

Let us examine the orders that Jesus Christ left for Christians, His "Great Commission," given to His disciples and individuals. He expresses that the best way to spread the Gospel is by word of mouth, one individual to another.

I wholeheartedly believe that it is a blessed thing to preach the Gospel to as many as we can, whether you are at a revival crusade preaching to thousands, or a preacher addressing a congregation. However, a group or congregation can only fulfill the Great Commission's requirements if, in the Sunday School class, or in the church congregation, there are poor, lost individuals who need to hear the Gospel. Every preacher's role is to preach to individuals, not a crowd.

The Soul-winner's Toolbox

We are not called primarily to preach sermons. We are called to share the truth about salvation. In some cases, sermons will help do that; in other cases, individual contact is the only way we can lead people to salvation.

"One of the two disciples who heard John's words and began to follow Jesus was a man named Andrew. He first found his brother, Simon Peter, and told him, "We have found the Anointed One! (which is translated, the Christ, Messiah) Then Andrew brought Simon to meet Jesus. (John 1:40-43, 45 NKJV)"

Jesus called Phillip and Nathaniel

"The next day, Jesus decided to go to Galilee, where he found Philip. Jesus said to him "come and follow me. (John 1: 43 & 45a NKJV)"

"Philip went to look for his friend, Nathaniel, and told him **"We've found him"! We've found the one we've been waiting for!**

This was good news that John's disciples heard, and the first thing they did was respond positively. Both Andrew and Philip went looking for their family and friends to share the news. Notice that the individuals did not keep the news to themselves.

"How beautiful on the mountains are the feet of those who bring news, who proclaim peace, who bring good tidings. (Isaiah 52:7a)"

"What a beautiful sight to behold-the precious feet of the messenger coming over the mountains to announce good news! He comes to refresh us with wonderful news, announcing salvation to zion "Your Might God reigns, (Isaiah 52:7 TPT)"

That refreshing news was long awaited by the disciples. Philip announced to Nathaniel, "We have found Him!" Will you announce the good news to others? Personal evangelism is sharing the message of Jesus Christ with others; it is showing and telling about Christ through words and deeds, who He is and how it's possible to have a relationship with Him. Think of evangelism in light of life's journeys. Personal evangelism is the privilege of entering into the spiritual journey of another person, discovering how God is at work, and understanding the role we can play.

We see through the scriptures above how Andrew first found his brother Simon Peter and told him about the Messiah. It sounds so simple in theory. Why do so many of us find it hard?

Christians may find it difficult to evangelize for various reasons. Some common challenges include:

- **Fear:** Sharing faith can be intimidating, and there's often a fear of rejection or confrontation.
- **Ignorance:** Some may want to share their faith but don't know what to say or how to start the conversation.
- **Arrogance:** A belief that one is above sharing the Gospel, thinking it's someone else's job.
- **Apathy:** A lack of concern or interest in sharing faith with others.
- **Bad Theology:** Misunderstandings about the nature of evangelism or the message of the Gospel itself.

These challenges can be compounded by cultural barriers, lack of confidence, and changes in society's attitude toward religion. However, we can overcome these challenges by:

- **Recognising where fear comes from:** Understand that fear in the context of evangelism is not from God and can often be a natural response to stepping out of one's comfort zone.
- **Relying on the Holy Spirit:** Trust that you're not alone in your efforts and that the Holy Spirit can guide you and give you the words to say.
- **Knowing the Word:** Being familiar with God's Word can help you feel more prepared and less inadequate.
- **Obeying the Word:** Taking steps of obedience can build confidence and reduce fear over time.
- **Praying about your fears:** Bringing your fears before God in prayer can be a powerful way to find peace and courage. Along with practice and support from a community, these steps can make evangelism less daunting.

Evangelism is an act of worship to God. When we share the Gospel, we declare His glory among His people.

The Soul-winner's Toolbox

"O worship the Lord in the beauty of holiness: fear before him, all the earth... say among the heathen that the Lord reigneth.(Psalms 96:9-10 NKJV)"

We are to tell the world that the Lord, Yahweh the Self Existing One rules over all!

As believers, we are called to worship God in the presence of all nations and people, declaring the characteristic and act of God in regard to salvation. Ensuring that the central focus, God. He defines the purpose and order of worship, inviting all nations and people to respond and join in.

This is our motivation as believers; when we genuinely desire to share our faith, the very thought can both excite and terrify us.

"For we cannot but speak the things which we have seen and heard, (Acts 4: 20 NKJV)"

The desire to share faith is a natural overflow of a person's relationship with Christ. Just as someone in love rarely stops thinking and talking about the object of their love, a person who has genuinely experienced Jesus Christ feels a similar compulsion. Sharing Jesus is always at the forefront of their mind, with a constant search for open doors to step through and share the gospel.

"There's an amazing door of opportunity standing wide open for me to minister here. (1Corinthians 16:9A TPT)"

"Furthermore, when I came to Troas to preach, and a door was opened unto me of the Lord. (2 Corinthians 2:12NKJV)"

So, we learn to look in every conversation for that door of opportunity the Lord has opened, where we can share with friends, colleagues, and loved ones. A door of opportunity symbolises a chance for believers to offer the listener a new perspective. But we won't know unless we open the door. So, when opportunity comes knocking, be ready to open it.

Nicole Bennett Blake

How do you know when the opportunity comes?

Let me tell you about one such experience I had. I had been out evangelising with others in the morning, and after finishing, I made my way to the supermarket. Standing in line to be served, I began to sing "The God of the Mountain." A young man in the queue turned to me and mentioned that he hadn't been to church for a long time but was planning to go the following day. I asked him which church he intended to visit. He didn't have a specific one in mind—just the desire to go to church. We began talking, and I asked what made him decide to attend. His response was that over the past few days, he had felt a strong desire to return to church. God had already prepared this young man's heart; I was simply the vessel He used to confirm His message. I shared the gospel with him, gave him my church details, and he agreed to attend.

This was an example of a door of opportunity opened for me to share the gospel.

"Always be ready to give an explanation to everyone who asks you for a reason for your hope.(1Peter 3: 15NKJV)"

Peter urges us to evangelise with gentleness, respect, and humility, delivered with clarity. We should openly share the good news of redemption.

Sadly, personal evangelism is not simply a process of explaining truth until someone understands and then automatically decides to believe in Jesus. People often have barriers or obstacles they must overcome before they accept the truth about God. God is more than a set of concepts to agree or disagree with. He is real, alive, and has shown us the one way our relationship with Him can thrive—by trusting Him as our ultimate authority.

It's not surprising that we, with our self-protective and independent instincts, often resist the truth about God.

But those who do not yet believe are only half of why personal evangelism can be challenging. If you are a Christian who wants to share your beliefs, you must choose to take a step of faith. You can't predict how the person you're speaking to will respond or how it might impact your relationship. Feelings of fear, anxiety, and nervousness are completely normal as you make personal evangelism part of your everyday life.

Many people would like to win souls, but they lack practical knowledge on how to do it. People who believe the Bible and sympathize with its teachings often want to win souls. Yet, when asked to use the Bible to clearly explain salvation, many may hesitate and admit they wouldn't know where to start.

The right kind of gospel preaching sends Christians out to win souls, touches the hearts of sinners, breaks through hardened ground, stirs the conscience, and creates a climate for personal soul-winning.

The Gospel Definition:

This is how the Apostle Paul summarised the gospel:

Moreover, Brethren's I declare unto you the gospel which I preached unto you, which also you have received, and wherein you stand. By this gospel you are saved, if you hold in memory what I preached unto you, unless you have believed in vain. For what I received I passed on to you as of first importance: that Christ died for our sins according to the scriptures, and that he appeared to Cephas, and then to the twelve.

(1 Corinthians 15: 1-5NKJV)

So, what exactly is the gospel? It is the good news that Christ died for our sins, was buried, and rose again on the third day, proclaiming salvation. The gospel is God's message. He is the author, and He defines its content. We don't have to create it ourselves; all we need to do is pass on the message. Jesus has already accomplished the work; we need only to embrace it.

Too often, we overlook God's sovereignty. His sovereign love provides the solution and enables us to receive His offer. Yes, we are responsible for how we share the gospel, but not for its content;

- God's sovereign love pursues us before we ever knew Him.

- His sovereign activity makes us aware of our need for the salvation He provides.
- His sovereign love continues to pursue us as we walk on the path of discipleship.

The gospel message has a beginning, middle, and end. The core truths of the gospel should not be altered or removed. This good news includes:

- Christ died for our sins.
- He rose again on the third day.
- He ascended into heaven.
- He intercedes on our behalf to the Father.

The message is about what Christ did, why people must be saved, and what they can do to be saved.

Cost of discipleship:

- It's a lifelong commitment with struggles; it's hard. We are called to die to ourselves, take up our cross, and follow.
- We must not remove the parts we find unsociable or unacceptable.
- We need to speak about heaven and Sheol (hell) and our life after this one.
- We are called to tell the truth, the whole truth, not just a part of it.

The Evangelist's code of Ethics:

Now, who will want to harm you if you are eager to do good? But even if you suffer for doing what is right, God will reward you for it. So don't worry or be afraid of their threats. Instead, you must worship Christ as Lord of your life. And if someone asks about your hope as a believer, always be ready to explain it. But do this in a gentle and respectful way. Keep your conscience clear. Then if people speak against you, they will be ashamed when they see what a good life you live because you belong to Christ. Remember, it is better to suffer for doing good, if that is what God wants, than to suffer for doing wrong." (1 Peter 3:13-17 NLT).

This is a mandate for what to expect when sharing the gospel. You should be eager to seek out what is good, spreading hope and love. Yes, you may face humiliation and suffering, but we shouldn't let that prevent us from going out and sharing. You should be ready to explain why you feel compelled to share the gospel. Our reason is that we have hope. Do it in a way that shows our compassion; we should be like a good physician, who wants the best for their patient but must deliver both the bad news about their health and the good news on how to fix the problem. "Yes, you have cancer, but there is a cure."

When you read the scripture, it does not suggest we should avoid going out. Evangelistic values guide believers in sharing the Good News with humility, wisdom, and love, even in challenging times. It encourages us to be prepared, gentle, and respectful as we proclaim the hope found in Christ.

Effective soul-winning means focusing your energy on fertile ground, where there is potential for growth, a hundred-fold harvest. Just as no wise farmer would waste valuable seed on barren soil that won't yield a crop, I believe careless, unplanned sharing of the Gospel is poor stewardship. The message of Christ is too valuable to waste on non-productive approaches. We need to be strategic in reaching the world, focusing our efforts where they will make the greatest impact, by engaging in deep, transformative conversations about faith and salvation.

In my book Evangelism Made Simple: 6 Easy Steps, you can find a more detailed outline of effective evangelism methods and an explanation of what evangelism truly means.

ENGAGING IN DEEP AND MEANINGFUL CONVERSATION

1. People invest time and energy into developing their careers, bodies, and relationships, yet often neglect the spiritual dimension of their lives. How do you actively engage someone in a conversation that encourages spiritual growth? When having a conversation with someone who has never heard about God, what would you share from your experience that might inspire them to want to know more? What open-ended questions could you ask to explore your listener's faith?

2. Let's take a closer look at the concept of open-ended questions.

Open Ended Questions and Closed Ended Questions: What Are They and What is the Difference?

A question can have many answers but some questions can only be answered with a "yes" or "no." Questions that encourage conversation are open-ended. Questions like "What did you want to be when you were a child?" and "What is your favourite food and why?" are examples of open-ended questions where your conversational partner is encouraged to explain their answer or reflect on the question. This creates a bonding experience and a shared discussion that validates the other person.

There aren't many interpersonal benefits to asking a closed-ended question. Closed-ended questions are more functional; they often serve simple purposes. Questions like "Can you show me where the office is?" can initiate a connection or conversation, but they don't tell you much about the other person. These questions typically have "yes" or "no" answers or brief, simplistic responses.

Open-ended questions encourage creative responses and genuine self-expression. With a conversation centered around open-ended questions, you keep the dialogue flowing by placing the ball back in the other person's court.

Asking closed-ended questions will usually lead to short and abrupt answers, unless you follow up with open-ended questions, such as:

- "Have you worked here for many years? What's good about working here?"
- "Wow, this gym is amazing! Do you come here often, and which personal trainer would you recommend?"

With open-ended questions, you can learn more about the other person and keep the conversation going as you get to know each other and build a connection. This is the beauty of genuine social exchange. Following up a closed-ended question with an open-ended one can help deepen the conversation.

3. Open-ended questions encourage genuine dialogue and self-reflection. Each person's journey is unique, and these prompts can open doors to meaningful discussions about faith and salvation

Here are a few open ending questions that you can use to start a meaningful conversation, to ascertain a person's faith.

We've never had a chance to talk about your religious background. Where would you say you are in your spiritual pilgrimage?

1. Have you ever come to a point in your life where you trusted Jesus Christ as your personal Saviour and Lord, or do you think that is something you're still moving toward? May I share with you how I came to that point?
2. Do you find that faith and spiritual values play a role in your work, daily life, marriage, or perspective on life?
3. If you could be sure there is a God, would you want to know Him? Or if you could know God personally, would you want to?
4. Bring a friend to your church or a Christian event, then ask:
    - What did you think of it?
    - Did it make sense to you?
    - Have you made the wonderful discovery of knowing God personally?
    - You'd like to, wouldn't you?
5. Do you go to church? Why or why not?
6. I would hate for you to come to my church and not understand what it's all about. Would you want to get together and discuss our basic beliefs?
7. We have been friends for quite some time now, and I've never really talked to you about the most important thing in my life. May I take a few moments to do so?
8. Has church had an influence in your life? Are you at a point where you want it to be a bigger part of your life? What prompted this? Would you like to hear our basic beliefs to see if they align with what you're seeking?
9. How do you think someone becomes a Christian?

10. Can I share what I've found most important to me as a parent, spouse, or leader?
11. What do you think about when you go to sleep at night? (If they mention anxiety or guilt, introduce the peace found in a relationship with Christ.)
12. Many people say they believe in God. What does believe in God mean to you?
13. Before I came to know Christ personally, God was a vague concept I couldn't relate to or grasp. How would you describe your view of God? Jesus? Is He a reality to you or more of an abstract concept?
14. If you were to die tonight, are you sure you'd go to heaven? Has anyone ever explained how you can know for sure?
15. I would like to tell you how I developed a personal relationship with God. (Share your personal testimony of how you became a Christian in three minutes, following this outline: Before—What characterized my life before I trusted Christ. During—How I came to trust Christ. After—How I am different now.)

Practice these questions with another Christian first to get a sense of where such conversations might lead and to build your confidence. Then, pray together, asking God to give you the boldness to ask some of your friends who have yet to believe these thought-provoking questions.

People are more open to spiritual truth at certain times than others. Many factors influence spiritual receptivity, and God uses a variety of tools to soften hearts and prepare people to be saved.

May "Doing It Jesus' Way" ignite a fire within us, sparking a passion to win souls, heal hearts, and extend the Kingdom. As we follow in His footsteps, we embark on the greatest adventure: partnering with the Saviour to rescue the lost.

We are never alone. The One who walked the hills of Judea still walks with us.

Here, I want to offer some practical suggestions for the soul winner's approach, character, and strategies: to show those who are lost their need for salvation, guide them on how to be saved, and encourage them to claim the Saviour.

"Hearts Wide Open: Reaching the Receptive"

In this section, we explore the beauty of encountering hearts ready to receive the Gospel—those who lean in, ask questions, and hunger for truth. Let's dive into the dynamics of connecting with receptive souls and nurturing their journey of faith.

There are seasons when people are more receptive to listen to the Gospel. God often uses emotional pain to draw people's attention through experiences like divorce, the loss of a loved one, unemployment, or financial troubles. People are also more receptive during significant life changes, such as a new marriage, the birth of a child, moving to a new home, starting a new job, or entering a new school.

God works through both change and pain to prepare hearts and make them receptive to the Gospel. When people are fearful or anxious, they often seek something greater than themselves to ease their pain and fill the emptiness they feel. A wonderful advantage of focusing on receptive individuals is that you don't have to pressure them into accepting Christ. "If the fruit is ripe, you don't have to yank it!"

Once you understand who your target is, who you are most likely to reach, and who are the most receptive in that group, you're ready to establish an evangelism strategy. My suggestion to you is this: start by checking the soil.

Identifying spiritually receptive hearts in your community is essential for effective evangelism. Here are practical ways to recognize those who are open to hearing the Gospel:

1. **People in Transition:**
   - Major life changes, whether positive or negative, often create spiritual hunger. Look for individuals experiencing transitions such as new marriages, new jobs, moving to a new area, or welcoming a new baby. These moments of change can make hearts more receptive to spiritual matters.

2. **People Under Tension:**
   - Emotional pain and stress can soften hearts. People facing divorce, grief, financial struggles, loneliness, or family difficulties may be more open to seeking answers and finding hope. Be attentive to those going through challenging times.

3. **Active Listeners:**
   - Pay attention to those who ask questions about faith, spirituality, or purpose. Curiosity often indicates openness. Engage in meaningful conversations with those who genuinely seek answers. Notice your unsaved friend who eagerly spends time in your company. For instance, if your lunch break involves reading Scripture, praying, or listening to gospel music, it's an indication that your friend is interested and eager to know more.

4. **Seekers of Stability:**
   - People crave stability amid a changing world. When everything feels uncertain, they look for "islands of stability." Share the unchanging truth of the Gospel with those seeking spiritual stability.

5. **Responsive to Kindness:**
   - Notice those who respond positively to acts of kindness. Compassion and love can soften hearts. Show Christ's love through practical actions and observe how people react.

6. **Openness to Conversations:**
   - Some individuals willingly engage in discussions about faith, philosophy, or life's purpose. They may attend community events, workshops, or gatherings related to spiritual topics. Connect with them.

7. **Attenders of Community Events:**
   - Attend local events, workshops, or seminars related to faith, wellness, or personal growth. Observe who actively participates

and engages in discussions. These attendees may be spiritually receptive.

8. New Residents:
    o In communities with frequent turnover, people are often more open to building connections. Churches can grow faster in such areas due to the influx of receptive hearts.

Remember that spiritual receptivity varies, and God works in mysterious ways. Pray for discernment and sensitivity to recognize those whose hearts are ready to receive the Good News.

Taking the Next Step:

1. Provide receptive individuals with a Bible and other appropriate literature. Have some Bibles on hand to gift to the most receptive people you communicate with. If your church has provided you with gospel literature (tracts) or specific documents to disseminate, give them to as many people as possible, interested or not.

Lay out a plan with them. A person is not going to become spiritually mature and be "saved" after a five-minute conversation. What is the next step? What should this person do tomorrow and the next day to build and maintain their new interest in your faith? Where might you direct them?

Consider exchanging information or providing literature about your church if you do not feel comfortable giving them your personal contact information.

2. Pray with them. If the person has never prayed before, they might be curious and nervous about the process. You can help facilitate this by walking them through their first prayer session. Offer a simple and brief prayer, introducing them to it as a practice. Explain how and when to pray.
3. Recommend a church in the area. If you are in a town that is not your own, take some time to become familiar with local churches

you can recommend. Knowing the time of the next service could provide a good next step for your potential converts.

"Go Where the Harvest Is Ripe"

Just as a farmer harvests ripe crops promptly, we must seize opportunities

Identify areas where hearts are open and receptive to the Gospel.

I believe God has called every believer to catch fish. It is always best to focus on reaching receptive people.

With this evangelism approach, you start your conversation assuming that the person you are speaking to is broken, poor, and in need of compassion.

Your main goal is to bring healing and encourage the person.

In the vast fields of life, where souls sway like golden wheat, there lies a sacred invitation to venture where the harvest is ripe. Let us heed this call, for the time is now, and the labourers are few.

1. **Lift Your Eyes:**
    - Look beyond the ordinary, beyond the mundane routines and bustling streets. Lift your eyes to the hearts hungering for truth, the souls thirsting for grace. They stand ready, waiting for the reaper's touch.

2. **Tread the Path:**
    - Step into the fields where conversations bloom like wildflowers. Approach the seekers, the questioners, and the weary wanderers. Their hearts beat with curiosity, their minds open to eternity.

3. **Bring Your Sickle:**
    - Carry the sickle of compassion, sharp and ready. It is not a weapon but a tool of love. Gather the sheaves of hope and bind them with threads of kindness. The harvest awaits.

4. **Press the Grapes:**
    - Enter the winepress, where tears mix with joy. Crush the grapes of doubt, fear, and brokenness. The vats overflow with redemption. Pour out the sweet wine of salvation.

5. **For Their Wickedness Is Great:**
    - See beyond the surface, beneath the masks and facades. Their wickedness is great, but grace abounds. The Gospel pierces darkness and transforms hearts. Be the bearer of this light.

6. **Go, Get You Down:**
    - Descend from comfort zones, from ivory towers and safe havens. Walk the dusty roads, sit at the well, and break bread with sinners. The harvest beckons from humble places.

7. **The Reapers Are Few:**
    - Join the labourers, few but fervent. Shoulder to shoulder, we reap together. The sun sets, shadows lengthen, yet hope rises. We are co-workers with the Divine Harvester.

So, my fellow reaper, go where the harvest is ripe. The fields stretch wide, and the ears of wheat bow low. The Spirit whispers, "Now." And in this sacred now, eternity unfolds.

Put ye in the sickle, for the harvest is ripe, come, get down, for the press is full, the fats overflow: for their wickedness is great, (Joel 3:13). Evangelism is about changing lives.

Nicole Bennett Blake

Changing Lives One Soul at A Time

The harvest is riper than you think! Jesus tells us that the harvest is good and amazing, inviting us to see the current harvest through His eyes. Let's delve into this fantastic parable and allow Jesus to shape our perspective on the harvest.

Jesus instructs His disciples, "The harvest is plentiful, but the labourers are few; therefore, pray earnestly to the Lord of the harvest to send labourers into His harvest" (Matthew 9:37-38 NKJV). Our Lord anticipates a great harvest not of grain, but of souls. But how can there be a harvest if no one hears the Gospel?

It is nothing short of astonishing, in my view, that just as Jesus tells His disciples to pray for more workers, He answers His own plea. In Matthew 10, Jesus responds to that prayer, sending His disciples out and granting them the authority to preach that the kingdom of heaven is at hand. This vocation is serious business.

At the end of the Gospel, Jesus again confers authority upon His disciples, mandating them to baptise and teach all nations everything He had taught them.

These men, called to work in the harvest fields, now share the same mandate: to baptize and teach in their respective areas. They are to share the Gospel so, that, through their preaching, faith may be ignited. They are to sow Jesus' message, planting that vital seed.

Many times, as Christians, we fall prey to the false notion that we do not count for much. However, this belief is not supported by what we read in the Gospels regarding Jesus' ministry.

If we ever feel tempted to minimize the value of the souls we encounter, let us remember Jesus' example of interacting with one soul at a time, which can inspire us to follow His lead.

Jesus told His disciples, *"Follow me, and I will make you fishers of men" (Matthew 4:19NKJV).* The implication is that if we are really following,

The Soul-winner's Toolbox

we'll be fishing – soul-winning. Jesus' last words were, *"Go therefore and make disciples of all the nations" (Matthew 28:19)*. The Christians in the New Testament went everywhere, preaching the Word (Acts 8:4).

How, then, can you and I be effective witnesses for Him?

Work does not get done without involvement. We can observe a situation and maintain positive attitudes, but it requires a willingness to personally engage if we are to put those attitudes into action. However, when it comes to the effort of winning souls, we can often feel intimidated. Sometimes, our influence can be as simple as reaching out to those we know and love who need Christ in their lives. The technique below is one I learned from the International Commission Missionaries.

Fears, Conversation starters and prayers:

For God has not given us the spirit of fear but of power, love and a sound mind. 2 Timothy 1:7	Many people do not share the Gospel out of fear: • They don't know what to say. • They fear rejection. • They are afraid to start a conversation with a stranger. • They don't know which scripture to use.

Nicole Bennett Blake

4-POINT CONVERSATION STARTER

A great way to start a conversation and overcome that initial fear is by using the 4-point conversation tool. Whether you run into an old friend, find yourself at the bus stop, are picking up your child from school, or are in the supermarket checkout line, you can use this tool to initiate a conversation and guide it toward a spiritually meaningful exchange.

> *Just remember these points:*
> 1 Greeting
> 2. How are you?
> 3. How can I help?
> 4. Can I pray for you?

If they respond with a "yes" to prayer, great! Listen to what they have to say and offer to pray right there. After praying, you can share your 15-second testimony and ask if they have a similar story about how Jesus changed their life. If they say "no," then share the Gospel using the Three Circles Model.

The Three Circles Model is a simple and effective evangelism tool. It breaks down the Gospel message into three key circles, making it accessible for sharing with others.

1. **God's Design:**
   - The first circle represents God's original design for humanity, which was good (Genesis 1:1, 1:27, 1:31).
   - In this circle, we recognize that God created us to have a relationship with Him. His design includes love, purpose, and fulfilment.
   - We were meant to live in harmony with God, experiencing His goodness and walking in His ways.

2. **Brokenness:**
   - The second circle acknowledges the brokenness that entered the world due to sin. Man, kind rebelled against the Holy God, and sin was brought into the world (Genesis 2:16-17 & 3:1-7).
   - Sin disrupted God's design, bringing pain, suffering, and separation from Him (Romans 3:23; John 3:36; 8:34).
   - Brokenness affects our relationships, our hearts, and our world. We experience emptiness, guilt, and a longing for something more.

3. **The Gospel:**
   - The third circle represents the Gospel of Jesus Christ.
   - Jesus, God's Son, came to restore what was broken. His birth, death, and resurrection provide the way back to God.
   - Through faith in Jesus, we can experience forgiveness, reconciliation, and new life. The Gospel bridges the gap between God's design and our brokenness.

Using these three circles, you can share the good news of Jesus with others. It is a powerful tool to help people understand their need for a Saviour and the hope found in Christ.

After my first introduction to this method of evangelism, within two weeks I practiced and memorized it. On the first day I went out using it, a young man gave his life to Christ. I had a small notebook and a pen; I drew the circles and explained each part. When I drew the arrow from the broken world to the third circle, where Jesus died on the cross, I added his name, symbolising his turning away from sin to give it a more personal touch. This works well; it also allows me to capture and remember the name of the person I am sharing with.

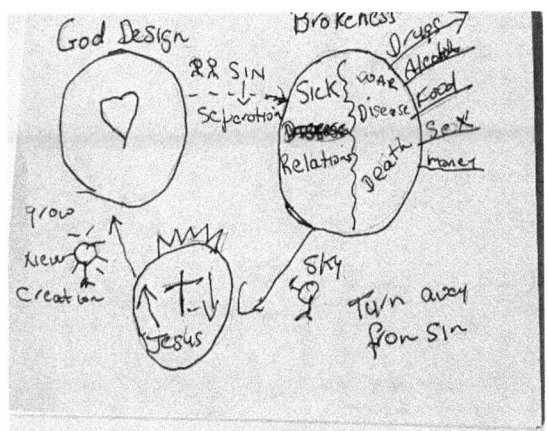

Answer any question they may have, arrange to meet within

24-48, after he had received Christ, left tract on 'The Free Gift.

Practice:
1. Ask God to give you an evangelistic burden for others.

Ask Him to help you see the world as He sees it, and to lay upon your heart a handful of people for whom you can earnestly pray. Then, pray over those names every day. Keep a small prayer list and pray for opportunities to reach these souls for Christ. An old song says, "Lord, lay some soul upon my heart and love that soul through me; and may I humbly do my part to win that soul to Thee."

2. Live a consistent Christian life before these people.

Jesus said, Matthew 5:14-16 *"You are the light of the world.... Let your light so shine before men, that they may see your good works and glorify your Father in heaven"*. We must live obedient lives of integrity and authentic faith. We must love when others hate and forgive when others harbour grudges. We must remain trusting when others panic and be honest when those around us are cooking the books. While we won't be perfect, only Christ was sinless; we should strive for a growing, maturing Christian life that others recognise and respect.

3. Build bridges to others.

When the Lord shows you those needing Christ, seek to build a relationship with them. Remember how Jesus went to the home of Zacchaeus, where many sinners had gathered? While we must be careful not to place ourselves in environments where we could be pulled down, we should also cultivate friendships with those who need Christ. Perhaps Christ has placed you in your community or workplace specifically to reach those whom no one else can reach. Take your unsaved friends to the movies, to a restaurant, or play a game of golf together.

How can we successfully reach the seemingly insurmountable goal that our Lord has given us to "Go and make disciples of all nations"? (Matthew 28:19 KJV).

We do this the Jesus way. Throughout scripture often Jesus made contact with an individual and meet the need that each individual exhibit. In so doing he is forming relationship with the individual so that he can best support their greatest need. Remember, in Proverbs 11:30 that says, *"He that win souls is wise."*

Daniel 12:3NLT says" "Those who are wise will shine as bright as the sky, and those who lead many to righteousness will shine like the stars forever."

4. Watch for openings to share a word for Christ.

If the right opportunity does not come naturally, create one. One thing I have noticed is that the unchurched are more open to church invites during holidays, as they often think more about spiritual matters. Take advantage of this openness to emphasise special invites during this period.

Nicole Bennett Blake

Do not wait too long in your search for just the right time to invite someone to church or share the message of the Gospel. There often comes a point when we must prayerfully introduce the subject and do our best to impress someone with their need for Christ.

John 4 records Jesus visiting a well, encountering a Samaritan woman. While she is hesitant to trust Jesus at first, the woman begins to believe He is a prophet, and the conversation turns to spiritual matters. When she learns that Jesus is the Christ, she runs back into town and invites others to simply come back and see Jesus.

In Mark 5, Jesus casts a legion of demons from a man, and those demons then drown a herd of pigs. Most of the townsfolk beg Jesus to leave, but the formerly possessed man begs to go with Jesus, instead. In verses 18-20, Jesus tells him to go and tell others of what God had done for him, and the man does just that.

These individuals all recognise the importance of the message that Jesus saves. They also understand the value of sharing that message. So why are we, as His believers, so focused on the right answers when our Lord Jesus is so good at asking questions and making people curious?

John 15:8 says: "Here in is my Father glorified, that ye bear much fruit; so, shall ye be my disciples." There are those who say that our prime motivation is not to win people to Christ but to glorify God. I do not disagree with them, but I must remind them that the Bible clearly says God is glorified when we bring forth much fruit.

During His earthly ministry, the Lord Jesus Christ won many souls for His Father in heaven. This is the reason the Father sent His Son, Jesus, to die for us. Jesus began His ministry through soul winning and, before He died, gave us the commission to share the Gospel with everyone on earth.

We should approach souls according to the individual, the time, the place, and the circumstances. Soul winning is an important part of our lives as believers because the will of God is that all people should be saved.

As Christ's representatives, we need to tell others how God gave His Son to provide a bridge back to Himself. When it comes to sharing the message of Christ, we can find meaningful opportunities in various contexts. Here are a few ways to watch for openings:

The Soul-winner's Toolbox

1. Sunday Readings Reflections:

- Explore "Opening the Word" videos and guides. These resources offer prayer and insights for the Sunday readings. Experienced presenters lead reflections, providing thought-provoking content for personal faith formation or group discussions.

2. New Year's Eve (Watchnight):

- On New Year's Eve, Christians often gather for Watch-night services. It is a time to reflect on the past year, commit to new covenants with the Lord, and look ahead with hope. Consider sharing a word of encouragement or a scripture or inviting someone to the service with you.

3. Conversations:

- Be attentive to everyday interactions. Whether at work, with friends, or in your community, listen for moments when faith-related topics arise. A simple question like, "How can I pray for you?" can open doors for deeper conversations.

4. Social Media and Online Platforms:

- Use social media platforms to share uplifting messages, Bible verses, or personal reflections. Engage with others in a positive and respectful manner. You never know who might be encouraged by your words.

5. Acts of Kindness and Service:

- Actions often speak louder than words. Show Christ's love through acts of kindness—helping a neighbour, volunteering, or supporting someone in need. I remember doing a podcast on my Facebook page, discussing how to evangelise by speaking to people you meet at the petrol station.

- A few weeks later, I received a message from one of my followers telling me that she followed my suggestion while at the petrol station with her husband. They spoke to a young man about salvation. The young man gave his life to Christ, and they shared the Gospel literature they had with them.

6. Invitations to Church Events:

Invite friends, co-workers, or neighbours to church events, Bible studies, or special services. Sometimes a simple invitation can be the beginning of a spiritual journey for someone. Remember that sharing the message of Christ does not always require grand gestures; it often occurs in the ordinary moments of life. Be open, sensitive, and willing to speak when the opportunity arises.

Romans 1:16. "I am not ashamed of the gospel; it is the power of God that brings salvation to everyone who believes".

The gospel carries divine power, it has the ability to transform lives and bring salvation. As soul winners, we proclaim this life-changing message with confidence.

The Soul-winner's Toolbox

WHAT MUST I DO TO BE SAVED?

Jesus and the Apostles gave us the blueprint (guided by the Holy Spirit) of how to be saved: one must:

			Romans 6:23
Hear and Recognise:	Romans 10:13-17	Romans 5:8	Acts 17:30
		Hebrew 11:6 John 2:30-31	Mark16:15-16
Believe with your heart: Acts 16:31 Romans 10:9-10 John 8:24			
		Matthew 9:13 Matthew 4:17	2Corinthians 7:10
Repent call upon God in Prayer Acts 2:38 Luke 13: 3-5 Acts 17: 30-31			
	Romans5:8	Matthew 3:6	1John1:9
Confess your sins to God / faith in Christ: Luke 18:21 Psalms 32:5 Proverbs 28:13			
	Revelation1:5	Acts 2: 38	Mark 16:15-16
Be Baptised Matthew26:28 Acts 22: 16	1 Peter3:21		
	2 Peter 1:5-11	Titus 2: 11-14	Colossians 4:2
Live a Godly Life	2 Timothy 2:15-16	Romans 12:1-2	1Peter 1:14-19
THE PLAN OF SALVATION:			

Why Should We Win Souls?

Many people believe that winning souls is solely the responsibility of pastors and church leaders. However, I disagree—we are all called to win souls, and we can only do so by sharing the truth about God and His attributes. Winning souls is precious to Christ, for we are all sinners deserving of God's judgment. In His infinite love, God sent His Son to save us, and He desires that we share this message of love with others.

God is a God of love, and He cherishes souls. This is why He sent His Only Son Jesus as a living sacrifice to bear the punishment for our sins. God values each soul immeasurably, and through loving Him, we learn to love others.

There is an urgent need to share God's love with all people, so they may hear the truth. God does not desire anyone's death or destruction. Instead, He yearns for everyone to come to Him in repentance.

Nicole Bennett Blake

Our love for God should motivate us to share His love with others.

Winning souls is the Great Commission, a divine command from Jesus to all believers to spread His teachings throughout the nations. This personal instruction calls us to step out in faith and share the good news. As Christians, we are compelled to obey this sacred commandment.

The Great Commission in Matthew we are to go and disciple and evangelise all the nations; we are to do it Matthew 28:19-20.

Every Christian is called to be a soul-winner, highlighting ways we can engage in this glorious and noble calling. Sharing the gospel is essential for the expansion of God's kingdom, and it is wise to win *souls*.

"The fruit of the righteous is a tree of life; and he that winneth souls is wise. (Proverbs 11:30NKJV)" Every believer is called into the ministry of soul winning.

1. *"They that turn many to righteousness shall shine as the stars for ever and ever.*
(Daniel 12:3NKJV)" We are called to guide others toward God's ways; the influence and impact of a soul winner endure beyond this earthly life. This path leads to the eternal reward of life with honour. It encourages us to be wise, to share God's righteousness, and to lead others to Him. Our faithful service will be rewarded with eternal brightness and honour in God's kingdom.

Joshua 1:9 "Do not be discouraged for the Lord is with you wherever you go" we are not to allow fear to hinder us, but it encourages us to live strong, courageous lives, anchored in God's unwavering presence. To face our challenges with faith and determination, knowing He walks alongside us.

Here are **compelling reasons** why every Christian should engage in soul-winning:

1. **Because God Commands It**:
   - Soul winning is not optional; it is a clear command from God. It is not merely a spiritual gift or a church growth program. We

are called to share the Gospel with others because God desires that all be saved.

2. **Because There Is a Hell**:
   - Psalm 9:17 reminds us that the wicked will be turned to Hell. Revelation 21:8 describes the fate of those who are without Christ. Our urgency in soul winning stems from the reality of eternal separation from God.

3. **Because We Love Our Fellow Human Beings**:
   - Soul winning is an act of love. God loves every person, and we participate in His mission to seek and save the lost. The most loving thing we can do for others is to introduce them to the Saviour.

4. **Because Souls Matter More Than Anything Else**:
   - Winning souls is not just a duty; it is a matter of life and death. We hold the key to eternal hope, and our efforts can change someone's destiny forever.

5. **Because Reconciliation Matters**:
   - We have been given the ministry of reconciliation. Going out to reconcile people to God is a privilege. When we lead someone to Christ, we bridge the gap between humanity and the Creator.

6. **Because Salvation Is Real**:
   - The Gospel message transforms lives. When someone receives Christ, they experience forgiveness, purpose, and eternal life. We have the privilege of being part of that miraculous process.

7. **Because Satan Hates Humanity**:
   - Satan seeks to blind minds and keep people from believing. Our soul-winning efforts directly oppose his destructive agenda.

8. **Because God Desires Disciples**:
   - Jesus didn't recruit spectators; He called disciples. Soul-winning isnot about mere conversions; it is about leading people to follow Jesus wholeheartedly.

9. **Because We Are Co-Workers with God**:
   - We join God in His redemptive work. It is an honour to be His hands and feet, sharing the Good News.

10. **Because Eternity Hangs in the Balance**:
    - Every soul matters. Our actions today ripple into eternity. We are investing in heavenly treasures.

11. **Because We Are Never Alone**:
    - Immanuel, God with us, accompanies us in soul winning. His presence both empowers and comforts us.

12. **Because It is Wise**:
    - Proverbs 11:30 says, "He who wins souls is wise." Aligning with God's purposes brings eternal rewards.

In summary, soul-winning is both a divine command and a compassionate act. Let us continue to share the love of Christ, one soul at a time.

Personal Reflection to raise why I feel called to Evangelise:

1. What is the scriptural basis for my call to evangelise?

2. Do I see reaching others for Christ as urgent enough to recognise the need to reach them now?
3. My greatest obstacle to effective soul winning is_____
   (If you are unsure, ask God to show it to you).
4. What steps will you take to overcome the greatest obstacle in carrying out the Great Commission to reach others?
5. On what do you base your salvation? _____
6. Are you currently involved in soul winning?
7. How long have you been involved in evangelising?

The Gospel: is often used to summarise the core message of Christianity, representing the following key truths:

- God created us to be with Him. (Genesis 1-2)
- Our sins separate us from God. (Genesis 3)
- Sins cannot be removed by good deeds. (Genesis 4-Malachi 4)
- Paying the price for sin, Jesus died and rose again. (Matthew-Luke)
- Everyone who trusts in Him alone has eternal life. (John)
- Life with Jesus starts now and lasts forever. (Acts-Revelation)

This summary is a way to memories and communicate the essence of the Christian faith.

Practical Tips:

4 Common Fears	Overcoming Fears
1_____	1_____
2_____	2_____
3_____	3_____
4_____	4_____

Many people want to win souls but may not know how to go about it practically;

1. One of the first things you can do to win souls is to develop a passion for them.
2. Pray for the guidance of the Holy Spirit; ask God whom He would like you to share the gospel with.
3. Have complete faith and absolute faith in your conviction about the finished work of the cross and a clear understanding of the gospel, so you can explain it thoroughly.
4. Carry a small Bible or New Testament with you, so that your audience can read the scriptures for themselves, or you can read aloud while they follow along.
5. Stay focused on the gospel; avoid arguments about religion or other debates. The goal is to point sinners to Jesus, who is ready to forgive and save them.
6. Show them the plan of salvation. Ask questions, and of the listener, if necessary, go over the message of the gospel again.

Self-awareness:

1. When going among strangers, whether on the street or from house to house, always go in pairs; Jesus sent the disciples out in twos.
2. When speaking with an individual, one person should lead the conversation while the other partner stays aware of environmental factors. Having a second person encourages confidence in the speaker and lends weight to what is being said. If your listener agrees to be prayed for, keep your eyes open during prayer.
3. A soul winner should always be mindful of their appearance; women should ensure their clothing is not revealing. A low-cut top or other distracting clothing may shift the listener's focus.
4. Practice good hygiene: take a bath to avoid body odour, brush your teeth, and check your breath. Carry mints or chewing gum to keep your breath fresh.
5. Demonstrate love to those around you, in your world. Don't be bossy; instead, be considerate and courteous. If they have children, show interest in the child. This technique has often helped me draw adults into conversation.

On several occasions, when I try to engage parents in conversation, I begin by interacting with the child. I smile at the child or start a simple game, like hide-and-seek, to spark their interest. Once the adult notices that I am engaging with their child, I ask a question about the child. For example, I might guess the child's age and discuss child development with the parent. Every parent enjoys boasting about their child, and if you're eager to listen, they're usually happy to share. I often mention that I teach Sunday school and share some of the interesting activities we're doing at church. This often leads to an invitation to church and further connection.

Chapter summary/Key takeaways

1. Effective soul-winning is about cultivating compassion and having a genuine love for people. We demonstrate God's love when we tell others about Him.
2. Develop the art of compelling storytelling.
3. We are all called to discipleship.
4. Be consistent in reaching out to people.
5. Ask open-ended questions.
6. The harvest is always ripe; God is simply looking for willing workers.
7. People are often more receptive to the Gospel when they face life changes.
8. God uses both change and pain to capture people's attention, making them more open to the Gospel. Stay alert for opportunities to share with others.
9. Present the Gospel simply and effectively. Remember, how you raise topics will depend on your personality, your usual subjects of conversation, and your unique style of soul-winning.
10. Trust in Immanuel; He is with you.

As we close this chapter, let us embrace the truth that we are never alone. The One who walked the hills of Judea walks with us still.

In this foundational chapter, we explore the essential tools every soul-winner needs. From prayer to understanding the Gospel message, we set our bearings for the journey ahead.

Remember, soul-winning is a vital task entrusted to all believers. As you engage in conversations, trust in Immanuel (God with us) and let His love shine through you.

In the next chapter, you will discuss the issue of fear, the role of the minister, the church, and the congregation, as well as what God's expectations are for us regarding evangelism. Consider the benefits of fear that propel us into acts of worship and ignite our confidence to Evangelise confidently.

Reflection:

1. What aspect of evangelism do you like most?

_____
_____
_____
_____
_____

2. How can you show more compassion in your evangelistic efforts this week?

_____
_____
_____
_____
_____

3. What steps can you take to grow in your confidence as a soul-winner?

_____
_____

4.How do you handle rejection or indifference when sharing the Gospel?

5.What Scriptures inspire and guide your evangelistic conversations?

6. How do you rely on the Holy Spirit's guidance during evangelism?

_____
_____
_____
_____
_____
_____

CHAPTER TWO:
HOW CAN I OVERCOME FEAR OF EVANGELISM?

Fear is a human condition common to each and every one of us; it often holds us captive and cripples us. In today's society, fear is a big seller, whether in the form of counselling or bestselling books. Fear dominates our lives; it is the deciding factor behind many of our decisions. Fear does not make you less of a believer; it makes you human.

It is okay to feel apprehensive about evangelising. Overcoming the fear of evangelism is a common struggle, but it is essential for fulfilling our calling as followers of Christ. Even the most seasoned evangelists experience moments of "fear".

In Isaiah 43 :1 we are reminded of God's promise *"But now this is what the Lord says—he who created you, Jacob, he who formed you, Israel: "Do not fear, for I have redeemed you; I have summoned you by name; you are mine."*

Here, we see God saying, "I have got this," and He gives His reason, "because you are Mine." This reminds me of the passage in Psalm 91:5, where God says, "Do not fear the terror by night, nor the arrow that flies by day. I will give My angels charge to keep you in all your ways." Then He says, *"The angels will hold you up in their hands; they will pick you up and carry you."* What beautiful imagery of a compassionate and loving God! This is the character of God. He not only knows you by name, but He also looks after you. He is your protector. He is declaring His love, redemption, and protection. It's a moment of grace and restoration. He said, "I am the Lord who created you."

Fear in the context of evangelism is a complex emotion that can significantly impact how Christians share their faith.

> *"There is no fear in love, but perfect love drives out fear"* (1 John 4:18a NIV). God's love, which builds our confidence, also banishes our fear and helps us see fear as a source of strength in evangelism. It compels us to take risks. Instead of allowing fear to consume us,

we can use it to humble ourselves and depend on Christ. Relying on Him for the right words, wisdom, and courage demonstrates strength in our relationship with Him.

For God gave us a spirit not of fear but of power and love and self-control.(2 Timothy 1:7ESV)"

"And who is it that will harm you if you become followers of what is good, (1 Peter 3:13)" Believers are protected by the power of God through faith for salvation.

While we may feel like fleeing when presented with evangelistic opportunities, we should not. We should not fear those who can harm our bodies. The gospel is the power of God; it is a rescue mission.

"Who *are kept by the power of God through faith(1 Peter 1:5)"* The gospel is the power that gives us victory and keeps us safe

Five practical steps to overcome fear:

Overcoming fear in evangelism involves practical steps that empower you to share your faith more confidently.

1. **Recognize Where Fear Comes From**: Understand that fear does not come from God. It often stems from our insecurities or from Satan's attempts to hinder us. Acknowledge this and rely on the power of the Holy Spirit to overcome it.

2. **Know God's Word**: Familiarise yourself with Scripture. Knowing God's Word helps you feel less inadequate or hypocritical when sharing your faith. Remember, you do not need to know all the answers; sometimes saying, "I do not know, but I will find out," is perfectly acceptable.

3. **Start Small**: Begin by praying for others or sharing a brief personal testimony. Develop different versions of your testimony (30 seconds, 2 minutes, 5 minutes) and share them regularly. Use phrases like, "That reminds me of something I recently read," and share Bible stories or promises.

4. **View Questions as Opportunities**: Instead of fearing questions, embrace them. Questions are bridges for effective evangelism. Clarify, open the Bible, or admit when you do not know the answer; this leads to deeper conversations.

5. **Pray About Your Fears**: Seek God's guidance and ask Him to replace fear with faith. Pray for opportunities to share Christ and build relationships with others. Connect with fellow believers who share your passion for evangelism. Encourage one another and hold each other accountable. Remember, practice and persistence will gradually diminish fear. As you step out and share Christ, you'll discover that people are more receptive than you imagine, and questions become opportunities for meaningful dialogue.

The fear of inadequacy is a state of mind in which you think your best is not good enough. First, acknowledge your inadequacy to God and lean on His strength because His grace is sufficient for you; His strength is made perfect in weakness.

Fear Not: Embrace Divine Appointments

Fear becomes positive when it drives us closer to God and compels us to reach others. When harnessed positively, it enhances and propels us into evangelism. Reverential fear in evangelism means recognising God's greatness, respecting His authority, and allowing that reverence to inspire us to share His message of love and redemption. Throughout Scripture, we are presented with numerous individuals who evangelised out of their love and reverential fear for God.

"Reverential fear" refers to a deep respect and awe for God. It means recognising God's greatness, respecting His authority, and allowing that reverence to inspire us to share His message of love and redemption.

It took me a long time to recognise or even admit to anyone that I was fearful of entering into deep conversations about God. I reached a point where I thought there must be something wrong with me; I was not a true believer. I began to question my faith, wondering whether I truly loved God or was simply going through the motions.

I started reading the Bible and searching for people who had, at one time or another, felt fear regarding their faith or in doing what God had asked them to do. This led me to Moses, who, despite feeling inadequate, carried out the task he was given by God. Moses trusted in God's plan when called to lead the Israelites out of Egypt. His faith allowed him to perform miracles and guide the people to freedom.

In the book of Job, we encounter a man who faced immense suffering and loss. Despite his trials, Job maintained his reverence for God. When God responded to him in Job 38–41, showcasing His power and ultimate authority, Job was humbled. His reverence for God was renewed, and he recognised that his own goodness paled in comparison to God's greatness. Job's restoration came not only in terms of heritage and fortune but also in his deepened relationship with God.

Job's story teaches us that even in adversity, reverence for God can lead to transformation and a powerful witness. When we approach evangelism with awe and respect for God, we become vessels for His grace and love, impacting others through our faith.

David: As a young shepherd, David fearlessly faced the giant warrior Goliath, relying on his unwavering faith in God. His faith allowed him to step forward and confront the giant. When fear threatens to paralyse us, we can choose faith over fear. Trust that God is with you, just as He was with David, and take courageous steps forward. David emerged victorious, demonstrating courage and trust.

Peter: Despite denying Jesus three times, Peter later became a fearless preacher. Filled with the Holy Spirit, he boldly proclaimed the Gospel, even before rulers and authorities.

Esther: She risked her life to save her people by approaching King Xerxes. Her reverence for God and willingness to act led to deliverance for the Jews.

Gideon: Gideon questioned God when he was unsure of the task or even the voice he was hearing. Often, we are told that we should not question God. My answer to that is, if I do not question God, how will I know the correct answer or be sure that what I am doing is His will?

One such occasion was after the death of my mother in law. I stood in my kitchen and asked the Lord, "What am I going to do with my time now?" I had cared for my mother-in-law for over three years, and now that she had passed, I realised I had a lot of free time and did not know what was next. God responded with three simple words: "Open air evangelism." I had no idea what that meant, so I grabbed my mobile and did a Google search. I soon realised that God was leading me into ministry to become an evangelist.

I did not act on this information; however a few weeks later, while in church and using my phone, I saw an advertisement pop up for a six-month course starting the following year. My mother-in-law had died in July, and now it was October when I saw the advertisement. I knew right away what I had to do. I spoke with my pastor, and he gave me his blessing to attend the course.

I am thankful for the training I received at Open Air Campaigners (OAC) in July 2019. They taught me to use the sketch board for evangelism, which has been effective in engaging an audience. Their motto is, "Present Christ by all means everywhere." Being part of Streetwise 2019 was one of the best investments I have ever made to build my confidence in sharing the Gospel. The knowledge I gained from that training has propelled me to share my expertise with others and conduct regular training sessions with my church and other churches in the district, both locally and nationally, as well as internationally.

These characters inspire me to face my fears head-on, not be ashamed and trust in God's strength and purpose.

"For he that shall be ashamed of me, and of my words, in this adulterous and sinful generation: the Son of man also will be ashamed of him, when he shall come in the glory of his Father with the holy angels"(Mark 8:18 DRB),

"For I am not ashamed of the gospel of Christ, for it is the power of God to salvation for everyone who believe" (Romans 1:16)

"The Lord is my light and salvation whom shall, I fear? The Lord is the strength of my life; of whom shall I be afraid? (psalms 27:1) NIV" We are children of light, and we are call to trust in God even in the midst of the challenges of life.

As believers, we should boldly share the message of the Gospel with others. We shouldn't be ashamed, afraid, or hesitant to talk about our faith. The Gospel is the good news of salvation, and it has the power to transform lives. When we share it, we trust in God's power to work through His Word, and as we share regularly, our confidence in sharing grows.

Through this, we come to recognise God's greatness, respect His authority, and allow that reverence to inspire us to share His message of love and redemption. It means not being ashamed to speak about God and His compassionate, loyal love towards us.

The role of the Minister/ Congregation:

Both the minister and the congregation have a crucial role in equipping believers to become soul winners. Ministers, by virtue of their teaching office need to do the work of an evangelist, faithfully carrying out all the duties of their ministry. The Apostle Paul did not call Timothy to the office of an evangelist but charged him to do the work of one.

"Do the work of an evangelist, fulfil your ministry. 2Timothy4:5b NKJV)"
An evangelist is literally a person who presented the good news of Christ.

Timothy, whether this was his spiritual gift or not, is being commanded to communicate the gospel as part of his ministry as a church leader.

Pastors and church leaders have the responsibility to preach and teach the Word to the congregation. Part of their ministry involves equipping members to share the Gospel and providing the necessary tools to support them in doing so.

This can be accomplished through various methods, such as in-house training, regular evangelism workshops, role-playing exercises, and debates on apologetics. Christians need to hear these teachings consistently and, over time, learn to articulate the Gospel themselves.

"But be doers of the word, and not hears only. (James 1:22NKJV)"

Equipping the congregation for ministry is essential, and when ministers are actively engaged in evangelism, their passion and motivation inspire the congregation. There is no greater joy than seeing people saved through the preaching and teaching of the Gospel. Churches may be strong in many areas, but if they are weak in evangelism, this must be addressed—it cannot be acceptable. Christians need to become active soul-winners.

If all other ministries, such as the men's department, women's department, youth group, and others, are active but the evangelism department is non-existent, this is a major concern. Evangelism should involve leading people to salvation, discipling them, teaching them, helping them mature, and involving them in the process of evangelism. This foundation should be at the heart and vision of every pastor and church.

Spurgeon said, "Soul-winning is the chief business of Christian ministry." Soul-winning is about reaching people, and it should be the pursuit of every true believer. This is the essence of the Great Commission: winning souls through evangelism.

The Apostle Paul says in (1 Corinthians 9: 19) says "For though I am free from all men, I have made myself a slave to all that I may win more." So, the question is, what did he want to win more of? The answer is that he wanted to win more souls. In his commendation, he praised the church in

Thessalonica because "from them the word of the Lord has sounded forth" (1 Thessalonians 1:8 NKJV). They had become missionaries by sharing the good news they had received with others. So, as we do evangelism the Jesus way, we will begin to make disciples.

Jesus says follow me and I will make you fishers of men!

Ministers have a responsibility to teach the congregation how to evangelise in the way Jesus did—reaching people one at a time, showing empathy, sharing meals, and meeting immediate needs.

One key piece of advice, I would give to pastors and church leaders is that every church must have an evangelism budget and hold regular evangelism training. Let training be part of every church's foundation, discipling newcomers into the ethos of the church.

Pastoral Role:

Anyone who takes on the role of training people in evangelism should hold a pastoral role within the church. They are not only teaching others how to go out and evangelise, but also how to engage in an ongoing discipleship program. Therefore, the trainer must possess a broad skill set in evangelism, recognising that no single approach will suit everyone.

Evangelism remains a personal endeavour, requiring each person to find and adapt a method they feel comfortable using. While stepping out of one's comfort zone is sometimes necessary, it's beneficial to be part of a church that offers solid evangelism training. However, if that's not available, it may be time to consider self-training to equip yourself. On the other end, you might be called upon to train others.

Whether you are a trainer or a trainee, we all must start somewhere and have a pattern to follow.

What key areas should a training program cover?

1. **Aspects of Evangelism**: Teach effective methods for sharing personal testimonies, addressing common objections, and handling rejections.
2. **Gentle Apologetics:** Equip participants with knowledge to answer big questions about faith, the gospel, and life.
3. **Special Services:** Provide guidance on organizing and conducting evangelistic events or services.

4. **Follow-Up:** Discuss strategies for following up with individuals who express interest in Christianity.
5. **Growth in Christian Life:** Offer support for ongoing spiritual growth.
6. **A Model to Follow:** Share general principles as a framework for evangelism.
7. **Memorised Gospel Outline:** Teach a concise, easily memorised gospel outline.
8. **Discipleship Nurture Group:** Provide instruction on forming and leading discipleship nurture groups.

Remember, each program can be tailored to meet the specific needs of churches or individuals.

Church Involvement:

Training is essential to achieving this, and one of the most effective methods is role play, where one believer takes on the role of the Christian, and the other as the unsaved individual. For ten minutes, the "Christian" shares the gospel with the "unsaved."

While ten minutes may not seem long, many Christians quickly discover they struggle to talk about the gospel for that length of time. The aim here is to shift Christians' thinking; people often say they don't have time for evangelism. So, the question today is, "Do you have ten minutes?" If, as Christians, we find it challenging to share the message of salvation with someone we know for even ten minutes, it indicates we could benefit from additional practice.

A core principle I teach in training is self-awareness and the impact of sharing one's own salvation story. It's essential to remember that your story is about what Christ has done for you the transformation that comes through a relationship with Him.

Long standing believers should partner with newcomers to help them learn to share their stories. Allow newcomers to practice a few times with a partner, alternating roles, before stepping out to share. Whether you're training yourself or others, invest in a program that emphasizes living a

Godly life. Soul winning is less about techniques and more about a life that flows from obedience to God and submission to His Word.

What is Godliness?

God has promised to complete the work in us (Romans 8:28-30). The Holy Spirit is the one who transforms our lives to reflect Christ's likeness. Godliness involves living a life that mirrors God's character and aligns with His Word.

Key aspects of godliness include:

Personal Development: Believers should engage in daily reading and studying of God's Word, fellowship, and prayer with other Christians. God has given us His Word, the Bible, so that we may understand His nature and how to live in fellowship with Him, and others. As we study the Bible, we learn about God and what pleases Him.

Speech: Set an example with your words by reflecting what God says. Let His Word shape your speech.

Conduct: Let your behaviour reflect the grace you've received. Live in a way that honours God and demonstrates His love.

Love: Show love to others, mirroring God's love for you. Love is a powerful expression of godliness. Jesus said, "If you love me, you will do what I command" (John 14:15). To please God is to show our love for Him. Studying the Bible regularly helps us know God more deeply and demonstrates our love through obedience.

Remember, godliness is not an optional luxury; it is both a privilege and a duty for every Christian. We pursue godliness by relying on God's grace and practicing it diligently in our lives.

What should be included in evangelism training:

- ❖ **Present the gospel clearly:** Emphasize clear communication of the gospel message.
- ❖ **Building relationships:** Teach the importance of authentic connections, as trust is essential for effective evangelism.

- ❖ **Living a godly life:** Provide guidance on maturing in Christ and reflecting His character.
- ❖ **Practice, practice, practice:** Confidence grows with practice. Role-play scenarios, share testimonies, and refine skills. Incorporate various techniques to suit different individuals.

Evangelism is proclaiming the gospel!

This is an area where pastors and church leaders may need to reconsider how they approach church activities and the work of evangelism.

Hindrances to Evangelism:

1. **Theology Overemphasis:** Too much focus on theology, with not enough emphasis on salvation and evangelism.
2. **Defeatist Attitude:** A negative belief that people don't want to hear the gospel, often used to justify a fear of evangelism.
3. **Self-Centered Leadership:** Reluctance to engage with unbelievers.
4. **Unrealistic Expectations:** Assuming that simply gathering as a church will motivate members to go out and evangelize, without offering practical encouragement and support..

How To be an Effective Evangelist:

"Meanwhile a Jew a man named Apollos came to Ephesus. He was a Jew, born in Alexandria, Egypt, and a terrific speaker, eloquent and powerful in his preaching of the Scriptures. He was well-educated in the way of the Master and fiery in his enthusiasm. Apollos was accurate in everything he taught about Jesus up to a point, but he only went as far as the baptism of John. He preached with power in the meeting place. When Priscilla and Aquila heard him, they took him aside and told him the rest of the story Apollos had been thinking about going to Achaia, and the brothers and sisters in Ephesus encouraged him to go. They wrote to the believers in Achaia, asking them to welcome him. When he arrived there, he proved to be of great benefit to those who, by God's grace, had believed. He refuted the Jews with powerful arguments in public debate. Using the Scriptures, he explained to them that Jesus was the Messiah.(Acts 18:24-28 MSG)"

1. He had an enthusiastic spirit and a passion for God, with a burning desire to share the gospel with others.
2. He taught the gospel accurately, even though his knowledge was limited. What he knew he shared with confidence.
3. He had a teachable heart and humble spirit, always willing to listen to those with more knowledge so he could expand his understanding and deepen his teaching of the gospel.
4. He was dedicated to building his faith and knowledge in God's Word, studying to show himself approved. Everything he learned, he put into practice.

"Timothy, do everything you can to present yourself to God as a man who is fully genuine, a worker unashamed of your mission, a guide capable of leading others along the correct path defined by the word of truth. (2 Timothy 2:15 voice)".

I admire how Apollos stayed within the scope of what he knew; he didn't stray into areas beyond his understanding. Sometimes, while evangelising, we're asked questions we may not have the answers to. In these moments, it's best to respond honestly, saying, "I don't have that information, but I'll look into it." This approach not only helps you provide accurate answers later, but it also deepens your knowledge of the Word.

Apollos also sought guidance from others, so when he went to new regions, he spoke boldly, engaging with fellow Jewish opponents in public debate and proving from Scripture that Jesus was the Messiah. He defended his faith with confidence. Often, we need to take a similar approach: learn a verse or passage, understand it, and even memorise it from different Bible versions to expand our knowledge.

This focused understanding can make our message even more impactful when sharing the gospel.

Encouragement to doing the work of Evangelism:

1. Focus on God's glory when preaching the gospel.
2. Bear fruit to prove discipleship: As John 15:8 says, "Bear much fruit, proving to be my disciples." We demonstrate our discipleship by winning souls for God's kingdom.
3. Remember that God chose us: He chose us, not the other way around, and we should have a deep desire to please and glorify Him.
4. Develop Christ's compassion: As seen in Matthew 9:36-38, we are called to share Christ's compassion for the lost, guiding them to truth.
5. Pray consistently: Pray for God to raise up those within the congregation with a heart for evangelism, as "the harvest is plentiful, but the workers are few." Pray that the message of the Lord may spread rapidly just as it did with you" (2 Thessalonians 3:1 NIV).
6. Preach evangelistic sermons: Deliver messages that stirs up the truth within people, inspiring a commitment to evangelism.
7. Equip believers: Show members how to evangelize. Pastors and teachers should equip the church, as Ephesians 4:11-12 instructs, training them to share the gospel in a compelling way.
8. Plan outreach events: Organise events that engage unsaved people with the church community. Evangelism is a team effort; as Paul says, we are to "strive side by side for the sake of the gospel." Leaders should actively participate to demonstrate the power of collective effort.
9. Stand firm in our beliefs about salvation: Regardless of societal views or obstacles, trust that the Holy Spirit has the power to overcome disinterest or opposition when we witness.

The soul winning church is a happy joyful church, because they are doing the work of an evangelist and it start with you.

Then you know that the Lord of the harvest as heard your prayer, and you are being empowered by the Spirit to share the gospel through the power of the Holy Spirit. His divine strength working through you. *"But you will receive power when the Holy Spirit comes on you; and you will be my witnesses in Jerusalem, and in all Judea and Samaria, and to the ends of the earth."* (Acts1:8NIV)

Our own strategies for winning souls will not get the job done. We need to pray to the Lord of the harvest the Holy Spirit, who will guide us to the right fruit that is ready to be harvested. Just as a farmer knows when and where to plant seeds and understands which types of soil yield the best crops, we, too, must rely on divine timing and wisdom. When a farmer plants corn, he expects a crop of corn. Similarly, when we plant seeds of faith, we can trust that the Holy Spirit will work alongside us to bring about a great harvest. The Holy Spirit is the witnessing power, and it is through Him that lives are truly transformed.

Pray that Christ will introduce you to the Lord of the Harvest!

"And all these things are from God who reconciled us to himself through Christ, and who has given us the ministry of reconciliation. (2 Corinthians 5:18 NIV)

"Therefore, we are ambassadors for Christ, as though God were making an appeal through us; we beg you on behalf of Christ, be reconciled to God." (2 Corinthians 5:20)

This verse emphasises our role as representatives of Christ, urging reconciliation with God. As ambassadors, we carry a message of hope and salvation, inviting others to turn to Him. Paul wants us to see ourselves as representatives of God and to behave accordingly. We are called to tell people about Christ we are ambassadors for God. Reconciliation is key to all that we must do. When we love people we develop a passion for souls. Jesus entrusted His disciples with the mission of continuing the work of an ambassador by showing others the way to return and become citizens of His kingdom.

"But as we have been approved by God to be entrusted with the gospel, even so we speak, not as pleasing men, but God who tests our hearts" (1Thessalonians 2:4NKJV)

As ambassadors, we represent and carry out the message and mission of Christ. We are sent to demonstrate His message of love, His attributes, and His salvation to a dying world.

How to get the conversation Started!

Let me ask you this?

How do you know when it is time to have a spiritual conversation?

Most Christians know that God has called them to be witnesses for Him and to share the gospel with others. But sometimes perhaps out of fear, perhaps out of preoccupation we miss opportunities to do so. Nothing beats consistently sharing the gospel one person at a time. Biblically, this is a process that should be taught and replicated one person at a time as well.

While not every Christian is called to be an Evangelist, but every believer is commanded to Evangelise!

I have always had a passion for telling people about God and bringing it up in conversation so that I can share my relationship with Him. It does not feel like a chore or an attempt to convince anyone to follow my example I just want to share the best connection that still overwhelms me to this day.

The Soul-winner's Toolbox

The Lord commanded us to proclaim the gospel to every creature. There are several ways to undertake one-on-one practical evangelism. It starts with a conversation. Often the reason people struggle to win souls is that they do not know how to start a spiritual conversation. It is so easy to start a normal conversation, but so difficult to begin a spiritual one.

The reason most believers find it difficult to initiate conversations springs from a place of fear. It's the fear of the unknown, of how people will respond, and the feeling of humiliation for a lack of knowledge and confidence in your speech, as well as the pressure of not knowing all the right scriptures references.

One way to overcome this fear is through introductions.

Start a conversation discussing the weather.

Compliment your listener on their dress style, perfume, or hairstyle.

"I love your perfume; can I ask what brand it is?"

These are all door openers to getting the listener interested in you and what you have to say. Everyone loves to be complimented and appreciates knowing that someone is interested in them and what they have to say. Take time to listen to your audience, show an interest in their story, and look for the opportunity to introduce Christ.

You might find yourself at any moment in a potential divine appointment, or prompted by the Holy Spirit to start a conversation with someone whom God has highlighted for you.

A light-hearted, gospel centered conversation about a chosen topic, can lead to a deeper, meaningful discussion about what following Jesus means to the listener.

The best way to overcome fear is to step out of your comfort zone and go as the Lord leads; start a spiritual conversation with someone you have just met.

The choice is yours: you can decide to keep the message of salvation to yourself, or you can share it with a world that is lost and in need of salvation.

Starting a spiritual conversation can be easy if you know how, but difficult if you don't have the basic techniques. There are a variety of ways you may do this.

These are some of the techniques I have used to start a conversation with a stranger.

The preferred method is to introduce yourself to the person you intend to speak with.

Hi, my name is_____ (insert your name) have you got a minute or two I would like to speak with you about salvation.

If the person agrees to speak with you then ask their name, and introduce your partner,

Explain who you are and your reason for stopping them.

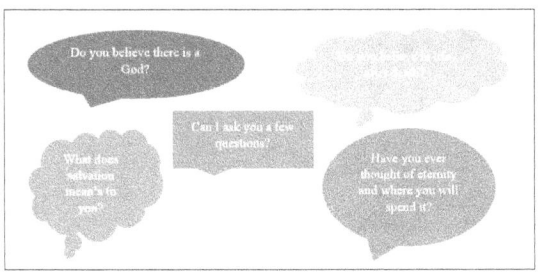

Base on the answer to question one you can then change your follow up question. Or get the listener to explain deeper their answer.

DOOR TO DOOR SOUL WINNING SCRIPT

Soul winning is the most precious experience you will ever have in your life. Door-to-door outreach is one of the most effective ways to win souls; it's a great way to reach people.

Often, people believe you are invading their space or backyard, which can make them feel uncomfortable in their own homes. They may think that door-to-door evangelism intrudes on their privacy. However, this is not the case.

Here are some tips you can use for door-to-door soul winning:

- When going among strangers, especially from house to house do it Jesus' way: go in twos. This approach ensures safety, accountability and follows Jesus' example of sending the disciples out in pairs.

- If you are going to evangelise by visiting people's homes, it is always best to go with a partner—preferably a male and a female. I do not recommend going alone. When going out with a partner, designate one person as the speaker while the other listens and keeps watch. Typically, one person should do the talking while the other ensures there are no interruptions.
- Ring the doorbell once, and if you do not get a response, you may want to knock once.

- Stand where they can see you when the door opens (hinge side) and when they look through the peephole.
- Speak immediately when the door opens or when someone asks through the door, "Who is it?" Silence works against you.
- It is helpful to start with an apology, regardless of the time of day, as this helps with the reception you will receive.
- Start with an apology: "I'm sorry for coming by so early/late; I hope I'm not interrupting."
- Who? "Hi, my name is _____ and this is _____."
- What? "We are with _____."
- If invited inside, wait to be seated. The nominated speaker should sit with the homeowner, while the other partner remains vigilant. Be aware that you are in a stranger's house, and the situation can change at any time. Never close your eyes to pray; keep your prayer short and focused on the specific needs of the listener. Your partner should closely observe the listener's body language.
- You are in an unfamiliar environment, there to give encouragement and moral support to the speaker while praying with your eyes open.
- Use open-ended generic questions, such as: "Have you ever heard about Jesus?" "What do you think of Jesus?" "Are you able to attend church anywhere?" "Where is that?" "Have you ever heard the Gospel?" "What do you think of it?".
- Have your church details and contact number readily available to leave with them in case of an emergency. Let them know they can contact you for prayer anytime they feel the need. This is a great way to break the ice during door-to-door outreach.
- Knock on the door and introduce yourself by saying, "I'm not a Jehovah's Witness or a salesperson (smile at this point). Introduce your partner first, then yourself. Remember, you

have already broken the ice; they may be more suspicious of the person behind you.

Say you are in the neighbourhood to see if you can help people this gets your foot in the door. (Do not ask to pray at this point unless this is the method you are using.)

1. Knock on the door and introduce yourself to your neighbour. Let them know you are in the neighbourhood to bless people. This will pique their curiosity.
2. Ask them if they need a miracle in their life.
3. You can mention that you are giving away free gifts of healing and say, "My partner here has an amazing gift of healing, and we are checking to see if anyone has any pain we can pray for and ask God to take away.
4. If they say they do not have any pain or do not need any healing, respond with, "I don't need anything.
5. You can say, "Great! Before I go this is what I see about you," and begin to prophesy the promises of God in their life. Share that God has a future filled with hope for them. If possible, share a scripture verse from memory, such as John 3:16 or Jeremiah 29:11. This will open the door for a deeper, more meaningful conversation about salvation.

Perhaps on the next visit the silent partner should take over. One person should do the talking, as a rule.

Keep a Gospel tract and your church contact details readily available to leave with anyone who is rushing and unable to have a conversation.

Here are some ideas for using tracts:

More and more Christians have used Gospel tracts to share their faith, and you can too! Whenever possible, read what the tract is about and sort them into different categories. This way, when you share them, you can distribute the tract that relates to their circumstances.

- ➢ Always start with an introduction, and reason for wanting to speak with the person.
- ➢ Explain to the person why you are sharing the tract and witness to the person at the same time. If the person is interest, you could offer to read **the tract** or explain what the tract says.
- ➢ Ask questions about the information you have shared.
- ➢ Do any of this information relatable to you?
- ➢ Ask open ending questions that will cause the listener to think about and explore how the gospel is relevant.

Why use a tract:

- It is easier to start a conversation by handing someone a tract.
- You don't have to struggle with how to start a conversation.
- There is no pressure trying to express all the right words.
- It is reusable, and often read many times over even by others long after they've been given to someone.
- It is often referred to as the "silent preacher" and paper missionaries. Due to its ability to tell the reader about the gospel silently, privately and one-on-one.
- It is an effective tool for Christians to witness to others quietly and effectively about Christ.
- It is one of the staples of evangelism.
- Once you make the decision to hand out tracts a few times, you will find it becomes much easier/ second nature.

Five steps to using Tracts Effectively:

- ➢ **Choose gospel tracts that are simple but complete**. Be sure that the gospel message is plain, and Scripture is prominent.
- ➢ **Keep tracts accessible to you**. Carry some with you each day. Keep a supply in your car or home.

- **Offer the gospel tract in a kind, humble way.** I love to begin by saying: "Can I give you something encouraging to read?" A smile and a kind tone go a long way.
- **Give tracts at appropriate times.** Look for every opportunity you can but remember that every circumstance is different. Often when I am in line, I may say to someone who is helping me, "I wanted to give you something good to read when you get a break later." Always be polite and courteous.
- **Explain tract**: when possible, read tract to listener and explain what it means, walk someone through a gospel tract and explain the way of salvation.

I am convinced that this is one of the greatest tools at our disposal for the advancement of the Gospel! It is something *everyone* can do.

Like any tool, Gospel tracts can be used effectively or ineffectively.

There are countless ways and places to hand out tracts, but the most important thing is for you to simply "do it!"

It is always about how we can make the most of our opportunities.

Here are a few ideas and suggestions:

Start with prayer. Ask God to prepare your heart to do His will and to direct you to the right person to give your tract to at the right time and in the right way.

Handing out tracts can be a key aspect of your evangelism, but it doesn't have to be. Keeping a tract or two handy in your bag, purse, or pocket is always helpful.

You can hand them to your postal worker and other tradespeople who visit your home.

Use opportunities at the post office, bus station, train station, or checkout stands.

Place them in your outgoing mail, including birthday and other celebration cards.

You can also give them to other religious groups that visit your neighbourhood, offering one of yours in return.

Handing out tracts can happen naturally throughout your day.

Make a pledge or commitment to distribute a specific number of tracts each day or week. Be intentional!

God will always provide opportunities for you to share the Gospel if you are willing to obey His command. Tracts are a valuable way to reach a vast number of people in the world around you.

3. Using Questionnaire:

- Complete a questionnaire based on the time of year. Go out in pairs, introduce yourself and your partner, and conduct the survey according to the season. Designate one person to do the speaking before you start evangelizing, while the other prays. The experienced person should begin, and after several opportunities, the less experienced partner can give it a try.

- Have several revised open-ended questions prepared.

- If you are in a mixed pair, the female could speak to women and the male to men.

Easter provides a wonderful opportunity for evangelistic conversations. Here are seven conversation starter questions that can open the door to deeper discussions about spiritual matters:

Questionnaire for Easter

1. What does your family do on Easter Sunday?

   o This question allows you to learn about their family traditions related to Easter.

2. Why does your family celebrate Easter in that way?

   o Understanding the reasons behind their Easter practices can lead to meaningful conversations.

3. Do you ever go to church on Easter? Why or why not?

   o Explore their experiences with attending church during this season.

4. Would you like to join me at church this Sunday?

   o Extend a warm invitation to attend an Easter service together.

5. Do you believe in God? What do you think God is like?

   o Dive into their beliefs about God and engage in a thoughtful discussion.

6. Are your beliefs about God the same as your parents'?

   o This question can reveal how their upbringing has influenced their faith.

Remember, Easter conversations can happen naturally in everyday life. Be open to divine appointments and promptings from the Holy Spirit to engage in deeper discussions with those around you.

Conversation starter:

One way of getting over this fear is through introduction.

Hello, I am conducting a survey on Easter to gather people's views and thoughts on the holiday. Seasons of events, for example, provide opportunities for evangelistic conversations in the course of everyday life.

Introduction followed by:

- Do you have a few minutes to talk?
- Christians observe Good Friday as the day when Jesus was crucified on the cross. What do you think is the significance of His death?
- Christians celebrate Easter Sunday as the day when Jesus rose from the dead. Do you believe in the resurrection of Jesus? Why or why not?
- If not, what would it take to convince you that Jesus rose from the dead?
- The same can be done for Christmas, Valentine's Day, Mother's Day, and other seasonal holidays. If you are visiting a new area, you could conduct a questionnaire about people's views on the area, park, or amenities, using this as a tool to engage in deeper conversations.
- These are examples of questions you could ask your audience to invite them to church. This will only happen if you muster the courage to start a conversation with strangers you meet at the supermarket, gas station, or wherever you go.

Start a conversation about the price of items.

- Observe how the supermarket is laid out, noting the constant rearrangement of the store.

- Compare the service you receive at this supermarket with that of another.
- At the service station or petrol station, start a conversation.
- Discuss the current price of petrol.
- Consider which type of car consumes the most petrol.
- Explore which car offers the best mileage for the dollar spent on petrol.

This method can be duplicated at restaurants or any other institute you visit.

Word of caution: The silent partner should never interrupt, and both partners should avoid speaking at the same time, as this can lead to unproductive discussions or arguments. Always ask for permission before praying for someone; never assume they want you to pray for them. The same principle applies to physical contact or entering someone's personal space.

Evangelism should not be limited to people we already like; it should also extend to those we don't know. We should aim to share the message of faith with everyone, hoping to help them build a relationship with God. Witnessing others awaken to their faith in Christ as a result of your personal evangelism is one of the greatest joys you can experience as a Christian.

In John 5, Jesus went up to Jerusalem for one of the major Jewish feasts. He visited the pool of Bethesda, where he saw a man who had been sick for 38 years. Jesus approached him and asked a question.

John 5: 6b *"Do you want to be made well?"*

That one question was enough to initiate a conversation between the man and Jesus.

Nicole Bennett Blake

What are some questions you could ask to start a conversation?

Let's examine a few individuals in the Bible with whom Jesus engaged in personal conversations and explore how these interactions changed their lives.

Even though our Lord interacted with multitudes of people (Matthew 11:7; Matthew 12:15; Matthew 13:34; Matthew 15:10, 30-31; Matthew 19:2; Matthew 23:1), He never considered Himself "too important" to engage with one person at a time.

How encouraging it is to read about His nighttime conversation with an individual named Nicodemus (John 3:1-21), His encounter with a woman at the well in Samaria (John 4:1-26), and His personal interest in a man named Zacchaeus (Luke 19:1-10).

How surprised Zacchaeus must have been when Jesus singled him out from the crowd, calling him by name: "Zacchaeus, make haste and come down, for today I must stay at your house" (Luke 19:5).

There are several ways to undertake one-on-one practical evangelism, starting with a conversation. Often, the reason people struggle to win souls is that they do not know how to initiate a spiritual conversation. The fear of not having answers to difficult questions and scripture references can be daunting.

We often find it easy to start a casual conversation, but difficult to begin a spiritual one. The hesitation believers feel in initiating these conversations often stems from fear—the fear of the unknown, how people will respond, and the anxiety of potential humiliation due to a lack of knowledge or confidence in their speech.

Frequently Asked Questions:

1. Is it wrong to say I don't know if a person asks a question you do not have an answer to?

Ans: You are human, not God. It is okay to say you do not know something because, let's face it, no one on this planet knows everything. Only God knows everything.

2. I'm a little afraid of the responses I will get. How can I get over this fear?

Ans: It's a good idea to go with a friend. First, it builds confidence to have someone who also believes and can fill in any gaps in your knowledge. Secondly, you can laugh it off together afterwards if it turns out a bit awkward. You could also try going with a church group, where you can simply stand and watch the first couple of times to get a sense of what to say. Most importantly, remember that Jesus and the Holy Spirit are with you Jesus is worthy of our effort. At worst, if you are rejected, they are not rejecting you, but Jesus.

3. What do I need to do if the person is not really interested?

Ans: Badgering someone is unacceptable. When a person has clearly expressed their desire not to learn more, they have set a boundary, and continuing to evangelise is disrespectful and intrusive. You can simply say, "Thank you for listening. I'll leave you with this information to read at your convenience," and quietly hand them a tract before moving on to the next person. Then, pray that God will touch their heart to accept the gospel.

On many occasions I have been evangelising and encountered people whose responses have been, "No, thank you," or "Sorry, I don't have the time." I usually respond with "God bless you. This often brings a smile to their faces, or they respond with, "And you too!" I then ask, "Can I pray with you or for you?" This often elicits a different response. They may stop for a brief prayer, share specific requests, and allow me to pray a short prayer before continuing their journey.

4. How do I overcome my fear of lack of knowledge?

Ans: It is perfectly fine if you don't know everything. Not knowing something presents a perfect opportunity for learning and personal growth. Read more, listen to others, and pray for discernment. If you don't know something, allow others to teach you. Life is a journey of learning and growth; if you know everything, you can no longer grow as a person.

5. How do I get people interested in the Bible?

Ans: Most people are interested in reading material that aligns with their pre-existing interests or promises to provide the knowledge they need. One of the best ways to engage others in reading scripture is to get to know them. By doing so, you may discover personal struggles or areas of interest that the Bible addresses. This knowledge allows you to make connections and recommend relevant readings to the friends you are evangelising.

6. What if it seems that the person is not serious with you?

Ans: Be as serious as possible about your personal faith. Make it clear that a relationship with Jesus is not a personal myth, but the most fulfilling and life-changing experience one can have. However, accept that their inability to take you seriously may reflect their own careful consideration and the conclusions they have reached. They might feel exasperated by your continued attempts, which they perceive as annoying. In this case, know when to leave them alone. You are not on a mission to force others to think the way you do rather, you want them to realise what you know through joy, not annoyance.

7. Is it my fault if someone does not accept my testimony?

Ans: Never! Some people need to hear the message multiple times before they fully accept it. Consider yourself a part of that longer process!

8. How do I depend on Christ for evangelism?

Ans: Think of it as a partnership. You are the spokesperson for Him, but He is the One who changes people's minds and hearts. You are not tasked with saving souls—leave the results to Him and focus on sowing the seeds. Additionally, pray before and during your conversations for revelation on what to say; you may even receive prophetic words for the individual. If you feel led, pray for miraculous healing and the manifestation of the Holy Spirit. Be sensitive to His leading, as He may guide you toward someone to speak to.

9. How can I stop myself from feeling nervous before I talk to a person?

Ans: Remember that God is with you. Trust that He will provide the words you need to say and have confidence that those words will flow from you. Thank you!

You can start by creating a 'tract' of your beliefs. Then, go door to door in a neighbourhood and simply ask if people believe in Jesus. Alternatively, you can engage in street witnessing without a tract or go as a group to places where people often gather in town and pray out loud. You may encourage others to join you.

Remember!

- Evangelise for the right reasons. If your motivations are social or material, you are no better than a salesperson. The Lord is always reaching out to unbelievers, but you can hinder His work if you are a hypocrite.

- Proclaim the truth of the Gospel without favouritism or partiality. Do not rely on opinions, non-biblical doctrines, or traditions when explaining the Gospel of Christ to unbelievers or members of other religions or denominations.
- Evangelising is not for everyone. Remember, a person does not have to speak in the streets to hundreds of people. Instead, pray, study Scripture, gain wisdom and knowledge, and if Yahweh calls you, witness to one person each day.

Let's look at how Jesus deals with difficult questions

1. Let's examine how Jesus addresses difficult questions. Throughout Scripture, Jesus often did not provide immediate answers to those who asked Him questions; instead, He frequently responded by asking His audience a question. In Matthew 19:16-22, we see Jesus engaged in a discussion with a young man who wanted to know how to obtain eternal life. Jesus aimed to reveal the areas where the young man was lacking, ultimately guiding him toward self-reflection. Often that's all we need to do—let people consider the journey they are on and where it may lead them.

    - Jesus was exceptional at asking thought-provoking questions. He did not hold Q&A sessions; rather, He conducted Q&Q sessions. If you asked Jesus a question, He would often respond with a question

2. Luke 5: 33 when Jesus was questioned on the topic of why his disciples did not fast. Although Jesus' answer addressed fasting, he uses this question to teach a broader truth.

    - In the face of difficult questions, Jesus demonstrated wisdom and purpose. Let's explore how He responded:

1. Reasoning from Scripture:

- When confronted with hostile questions, Jesus often reasoned from the Scriptures. In Mark 12, religious and political leaders challenged Him, but He silenced them by appealing to God's Word. His answers were rooted in divine truth.

2. Redirecting Focus:

- Jesus did not always give direct answers. Instead, He redirected the conversation to deeper matters. He spoke openly to those with receptive hearts and indirectly to those whose hearts were closed. His goal was to lead people toward understanding their relationship with Him. In Matthew 15:1-9, Jesus responded to the leaders who wanted to know why the disciples did not wash their hands before eating. He asked why they transgressed the commandment of God with their traditions, continuing to speak about the command for children to honour their parents.

3. Inviting Conversation:

- Rather than controlling or manipulating, Jesus invited others into conversation. He asked questions, allowing them to reflect on their beliefs and their positions in relation to Him. His approach was both respectful and thought-provoking.

4. Defining His Identity and Mission:

- Throughout the Gospels, Jesus consistently defined Himself by declaring who He was and what His mission entailed. He did not shy away from His identity as the Son of God and the Saviour. His clarity helped others understand the significance of their encounter with Him.

In our interactions, let's follow Jesus' example. May we reason from God's Word, redirect conversations toward Christ, and invite others to explore their relationship with the Saviour.

Here are some Scriptures to Memorise for Soul Winning:

- Romans1:16 *"for I am not a shame of the gospel of Christ, for it is the power of God to salvation for everyone who believes...*
- Romans 3:10 *There is no one righteous, not even one;*
- Romans 3: 23 *All have sinned and fall short of the glory of God,*
- Romans 5:12 *"Therefore, just as sin entered the world through one man, and death through sin, and in this way death came to all people, because all sinned*
- Romans 6:23 *For the wages of sin is death, but the gift of God is eternal life in Christ Jesus our Lord.*
- Romans 5:8 *But God demonstrates his own love for us in this: While we were still sinners, Christ died for us.*
- John 3:16 *For God so loved the world that he gave his one and only Son, that whoever believes. in him shall not perish but have eternal life.*
- *For what I received I passed on to you as of first importance[a]: that Christ died for our sins according to the Scriptures, 4 that he was buried, that he was raised on the third day according to the Scriptures".*(1 Corinth 15:3-4)
- *"Herein is love, not that we loved God, but that he loved us, and sent his Son to be the propitiation for our sins. (*1John 4:10)

How to Do It: Practical Tips:

When engaging in one-on-one evangelism, following Jesus' example is essential.

Here are some practical tips for sharing the Gospel in a Christ-like manner:

1. **Make It Personal:**

   - Know Your Audience: Understand the person you're speaking with. Listen actively and show a genuine interest in their life.

   - Share Your Story: Begin by sharing your own faith journey. Describe how Jesus transformed your life.

2. **Choose the Right Time and Place:**

   - Natural Settings: Engage in conversations during everyday moments—over coffee, on a walk, or while waiting for public transport.

   - Respect Boundaries: Be mindful of the other person's comfort level. Avoid contentious topics or unsuitable locations.

   - Be Mindful of Personal Care: Always ensure good hygiene; consider carrying mints or gum to freshen your breath before starting a conversation.

Your Role
- Practice with a Partner: Practicing with someone else helps build confidence and prepares you for sharing effectively. Do this a few times before going out.
- Guide the Conversation: The soul-winner should generally lead the conversation.
- Handle Difficult Questions: If the person you're speaking with raises questions, such as why God allows suffering, why there are so many denominations, or mentions hypocrisy in the church, you might say, "That's a good question. Remind me to come back to it later, but first, let me share this with you."
- Emphasize the Importance: You are discussing the most important subject in the world. Plan ahead and have a few simple steps prepared to guide the conversation.
- Focus on Key Points: Lead the discussion through the guilt of sin, the salvation paid for by Jesus Christ, and the fact that this salvation is freely available to everyone who accepts Christ as their personal Saviour.
- Share the Gospel Year-Round: The Gospel can be shared in any season—Easter, Christmas, Valentine's Day, Mother's Day, Father's Day, and even Halloween.
- Embrace Life's Milestones: Share during times like bereavement, sickness, funerals, weddings, and christenings.
- Spread the Message Anywhere: Share while in the park, shopping, at work, commuting, at home gatherings, or at social events.
- Use Various Methods: Share the Gospel by speaking directly, leaving tracts in mailboxes, using social media, or giving out blessing bags.
- Reach Out to Everyone: Family, friends, colleagues, neighbours, strangers, gym buddies, running club

members, workmen, delivery people, and even customer advisors over the phone can all be opportunities to share the Gospel.

COMMON MISTAKES EVERYONE CAN THINK OF!

- When engaging in one-on-one evangelism, it is essential to be aware of common mistakes and avoid them. Here are some pitfalls to steer clear of:

- Not Being Yourself:

  o Effective evangelism does not require a specific personality type. God has uniquely gifted you to reach others. Be authentic, and don't compare yourself to others. Your experiences and personality matter God used Moses despite his weaknesses, and He can use you too.

- Overcomplicating the Message:

  o Keep the Gospel message simple. Avoid theological jargon or complex terms. Focus on key points: God's love, humanity's sin, Jesus' sacrifice, and the invitation to follow Christ. Don't overwhelm others with unnecessary details.

- Ignoring Boundaries:

  o Respect people's boundaries. Choose appropriate locations and times for evangelism. Avoid contentious settings or situations. Be courteous and sensitive to others' comfort levels.

Warnings

- If someone becomes argumentative while you're witnessing to them, consider saving the conversation for another time. Some people are only interested in arguing, not in genuinely hearing the Gospel; they may simply want to provoke you. Don't let them. Always stay calm.

- Avoid unnecessary arguments by respecting those of other faiths who are content in their beliefs. Standing outside other places of worship to evangelise invites conflict, so avoid this approach.

- For safety, it is ideal to go out in pairs when doing street witnessing just as Jesus sent the disciples out two by two.

PLEASE DO NOT

1. Walk across people's lawns—as a courtesy to them
2. Speak to children without parents' consent
3. Gaze into windows or letterbox!

Chapter Encouragement

1. **Reverence for God**: This type of fear acknowledges God's holiness, majesty, and authority. It recognizes that God is infinitely greater than us and deserves our utmost respect. It is not a fear of punishment but a deep reverence for His character.
2. **Motivation for Evangelism:** When we have a reverential fear of God, it compels us to share the Gospel with others. We understand that God's love and salvation are too precious to keep to ourselves. Our desire to honour Him drives us to proclaim His grace.
3. **Balancing Fear and Love:** Reverential fear does not negate God's love; it complements it. We fear disappointing Him because we love Him deeply. This fear motivates us to live obediently and to share His love with others.

4. **Evangelism:** Sharing the good news with others, presenting Christ in a calm and precise manner, as stated in 1 Peter 3:15.
5. **Why Evangelism:** "Go into all the Earth and make disciples of every nation" (Matthew 28:19).
6. **We Are Ambassadors of Christ:** We represent Christ on Earth. As we go about our daily lives, we are to embody the values of another Kingdom (1 Thessalonians 2:4).
7. **The Gospel:** We are called to share the good news of who Christ is and what He did.
8. **The Message:** It has a beginning, middle, and end. The essential elements of the Gospel should not be altered or removed. The good news is that Christ died for our sins and rose from the dead.

Practical Tips:

Steps for Door to Door Evangelism:

1.Start with Prayer; pray for Holy Spirit to be with you, guide you and strengthen you.

2. Go in pairs:

3. Introduce yourself and your partner

4. Offer to share a brief testimony

Chapter summary/Key takeaways

- God calls us to live out the Gospel and engage others in what we believe.
- Start conversations with a compliment about your listener's style, perfume, or hairstyle, or by making a light comment about the weather.
- For example: "I love your perfume; may I ask what it's called?"
- These are door openers that help spark interest from the listener in you and what you have to say. Everyone appreciates

a genuine compliment and knowing someone is interested in them.
- Take time to listen actively to your audience, showing interest in their story and watching for an opportunity to introduce Christ.
- Leave literature when no one is available to answer. Place it in a safe visible location or in the letterbox. Consider using a "Sorry I missed you card, which can be easily created, with your church logo details and a brief message.
- In summary, fear is natural, but it can be transformed into strength when we rely on God and actively engage in sharing the Gospel.

Key point.

1. An effective evangelist should have a solid knowledge of the Word.
2. Preach the Word of God accurately and boldly.
3. Be enthusiastic about the Gospel.
4. Be willing to learn from others.
5. Show humility, compassion, and love toward others.

It is your story that will add weight to your evangelising.

In the next chapter we'll learn how to wield our stories with grace and courage. Learn the art of preparation before even trying to evangelise, pray for those you will come in contact with. Acts 16: 13-15 tell us that Paul went out the city gate (a place of safety) looking for a place to pray. He began to speak to the women that were there. One of the women that was there was Lydia, and she began to listen to Paul … "The Lord open her heart to respond to Paul's message." Acts 16: 14b) as a result of her listening to the message she and her entire household was saved.

Reflection:

What was the last evangelistic conversation that you had?

_____

_____

_____

_____

_____

_____

Are you actively sharing your faith when natural opportunities occur?

_____

_____

_____

_____

_____

_____

How Will You Take Action?

_____

_____

_____

_____

_____

_____

How will you prepare to share the gospel?

_____

_____

_____

_____

_____

_____

PART II:
SHARE YOUR STORY

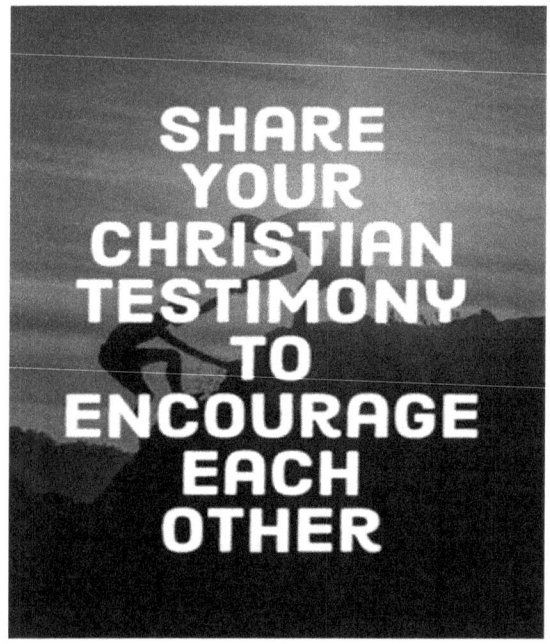

YOUR STORY IS YOUR TESTIMONY!

Nicole Bennett Blake

CHAPTER THREE:
UNVEILING GRACE: SHARING YOUR PERSONAL TESTIMONY

CHAPTER INTRODUCTION

In the quiet corners of our lives, where faith meets vulnerability, lies a story a testimony etched upon our hearts. It's not a polished script but a raw, authentic account of God's relentless pursuit. As we step into this new chapter, let us explore the art of sharing our faith journey the highs, the lows, and the transformative encounters with the Divine.

Sharing your Christian testimony with unsaved individuals is a powerful way to connect and testify to God's transformative work in your life. It holds immense significance. It's also an act of obedience to God's command, echoing Jesus' words in Matthew 28:19, "Go and make disciples of all nations." Sharing the Gospel isn't optional; it is a command for every believer. By sharing your story, you actively participate in fulfilling this divine mandate.

You are a living testimony. Only you can make your life a witness to God's power. Non-Christians observe your actions and character, and when you genuinely live out your faith, it speaks louder than words.

My own story may not seem as profound as those in the Bible. It wasn't marked by a major event, at least not to others. For me, it was life-changing. I had the privilege at age eleven, to hear about Christ, and being the inquisitive child I was I had to find out more.

I was fascinated by the idea of death bringing life and wanted to understand why that was so significant. My journey began at my church's vocational summer school, where we had missionaries from America. When they spoke, I wanted to be just like them. They broke down the

Scriptures and used stories to explain the Gospel in clear and vivid ways. I was captivated by the idea of having two fathers, even though my earthly father was an elder in the church, as the last born this means I would get more opportunities, and this would be something I did not have to share with my siblings. Being the last born of thirteen children, this means I would be have a heavenly father who would love me unconditionally and I had Him all to myself.

Returning home from summer school, I informed my father that I wanted to become a Christian, but he said I was too young to fully understand. He instructed me to read my Bible daily, attend church, and learn how to live a Christian life. This meant no fighting at school or getting into trouble. I was expected to live as an example of a changed life.

After a year both the pastor and my father agreed that I had passed the test and could be baptized. On Good Friday, at 5 AM, I was baptized in the river. It was the best day of my life. My family and friends were there to witness my new birth.

Looking back, it has been a challenging journey. I've stumbled many times, but God's grace has always been my Mulligan. He continues to work in me and through me, reminding me constantly of His unwavering love.

The Power of Storytelling:

Storytelling Power: Stories resonate deeply with people. Share how God has worked in your life, as your personal experiences can lead others to faith. They are a powerful tool to exalt Christ and draw others to Him. Let Jesus be the hero of every story you tell.

"They overcame him by the blood of the Lamb and by the word of their testimony." Revelation 12:11

Our testimonies are more than words; they are spiritual weapons. They dismantle strongholds, break chains, and ignite hope. In this chapter, we will learn how to wield our stories with grace and courage.

Remember, your Gospel story is not just about what you say; it is about how you live and the impact you have on others.

2. Crafting Your Narrative

- **The "Before":** Describe your life before encountering Jesus. What voids were you seeking to fill? What questions haunted your nights? I like to call this segment the "BC," or "Before Christ aspect of your life.
- **The Turning Point:** Share the moment when grace collided with your brokenness. How did you surrender to Christ?
- **The "After":** Illuminate the transformation. How did Jesus rewrite your story? What new purpose emerged?

3. Authenticity and Relatability

- **Be Real:** Authenticity resonates. Don't sugar-coat your struggles or gloss over your doubts.
- **Relate to Others:** Our stories connect us. Someone out there needs to hear your journey.
- People often perceive Christians as hypocritical. By living consistently with your beliefs, you gain credibility. Authenticity opens doors for conversations about faith, share your experiences honestly, including your doubts and struggles.

4. The Hero of Every Tale

- Point to Jesus: He is the protagonist—the One who redeems, restores, and rewrites. Make Him known.

God does not call the equipped; He equips the called. Depend on the Holy Spirit, just as Paul did, to guide your words and actions.

Romans 10:13-14 emphasizes that people need to hear the gospel. You become a channel through which others encounter the love of Christ.

5. Invitations and Seeds

- **Invite Others In**: Extend an invitation to explore faith by offering resources, church events, or Bible studies.
- **Plant Seeds**: Not every encounter leads to immediate conversion; trust God's timing.

6. Prayer and Preparation

- Pray for those you interact with. Ask God to bring people into your life who need Him. Your prayers can pave the way for divine encounters. Ask the Holy Spirit to lead you to the right person at the right time.
- Pray Silently: As you share, pray for the Holy Spirit's work in their hearts.
- Prepare Your Heart: Evangelism is not about eloquence; it is about obedience.

May this chapter embolden you—a storyteller of grace—to unveil the Author of our salvation.

1. **Practice Sharing**:
   - **Enthusiasm**: Share with passion, relying on the Holy Spirit.
   - **Speak Clearly**: Use a natural, relaxed tone, and avoid Christian jargon.
   - **Stick to Your Time Limit**: Be concise and avoid overwhelming your listeners.

2. **Invite Further Conversation**:
   - Ask Questions: Probe deeper. Inquire about their beliefs, experiences, and thoughts.

Remember, your story is a powerful tool to reveal God's grace. As you share, pray silently for the Holy Spirit's work in their hearts. We all have a personal story of how we came to know Jesus in a personal, life-changing way. You can use your testimony to spread the Gospel of Christ through personal evangelism.

The message of Christ is one to be shared, and we have some vast diverse ways to convey it. The most effective approach is to avoid pressing those who are closed off to you while persisting with those who are open. Listening closely will help you gauge their interest and open them up even more. This is a powerful way to impact lives and fulfil the Great Commission.

PRACTICAL STEPS OF HOW TO SHARE YOUR GOSPEL STORY

1. **Live a Godly Life**:
   - Your actions speak louder than words. Demonstrate Christ's love through your behaviour, kindness, and compassion.
   - Spend time with others meet their needs, and be a good listener. Let your life reflect the transformation that Christ has brought about in you.

2. **Pray for Opportunities**:
   - Pray for divine encounters. Ask God to place people in your life who need Him.

- Pray for wisdom and boldness to share the gospel when opportunities arise.

3. **Be Passionate About Christ**:
    - Cultivate a deep love for Jesus. Your passion will naturally draw others' attention.
    - Show that there is something different about you because of your relationship with Christ.

4. **Learn the 4 Simple Steps to Share the Gospel**:
    - **God's Plan**: Explain that God loves everyone and offers peace and life through Jesus.
    - **Our Problem**: Share that we are all separated from God due to sin.
    - **God's Solution**: Explain that Jesus died for our sins, bridging the gap between us and God.
    - **Our Response**: Encourage them to repent, believe in Jesus, and receive eternal life.

Romans 10:9-10 states, "That if you confess with your mouth the Lord Jesus and believe in your heart that God raised Him from the dead, you shall be saved. For with the heart, one believes unto righteousness, and with the mouth, confession is made unto salvation."

Be Relational: Connect with people in your daily life. Use social media, phone calls, or face-to-face interactions.

Below is feedback from several churches attendees to the evangelism training I facilitated during Lock-down.

1. Loving this discussion about how to tell your story: Stephanie

Nicole Bennett Blake

2. Life before Christ: How you came to know Christ life after you received Him: **Maureen**
3. Dress appropriately: Your personal story is important, so be mindful of what to share. Prayer is essential to understand the practical aspects and the importance of how we present ourselves: **Clara**
4. Personal story is important: Prepare, plan, and pray: **Clara**
5. I understand: For example, one cannot say they go to evil powers to get something, as that brings no glory and is devilish. In the company of unsaved friends, we need to be strong to handle situations like being in a club or a smoking place. If it can drag us back to our old lives, it's best to avoid those places and choose others to witness instead: **J.W.**
6. They asked: Sometimes we say we are children of God, and they disagree. But sheep give birth to sheep, so God gives birth to God and the Word says we are children of God not slaves of God. Thanks for the training; it was full of lovely, vital tools we needed: **J.W.**
7. Well done, Sis Nicole: Good teaching! I am empowered; today's training was enlightening: **Bev**
8. Thank you, Sis Nicole: Bless you! Well done: **Maureen**
9. Well done, Bishop Nicole: Very good: **Rev Daniel Barnet, St. Jude's**

Below is a testimony from a young man I met while sharing the gospel and he gave his life to Christ:

"I just met Nicole, and she spoke to me about salvation, leading me to accept Jesus as my Lord and Savior." **(L.B. 8/7/22)**

I also provided him with reading resources, and since he was visiting the area, I connected him with a church nearby.

Listen to Their story

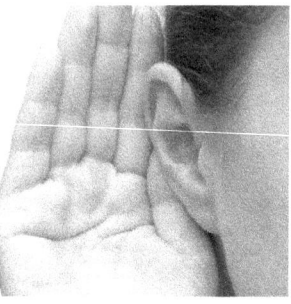

Everyone needs to take time to listen to their story because everyone has a story to tell. They will share how their life has been—whether good or bad, sick or well. They will express what they think of God. We must take this time to listen to their stories without being judgmental.

Listening to someone's story is profoundly important, especially when engaging with unbelievers.

Here is why:

Having relationships, human connection, and empathy are natural parts of life. As humans, we love to be listened to; listening bridges gaps. It reminds us that we are all part of the human experience, encouraging us to show empathy toward others. By listening to someone's story, we step into their shoes, feel their emotions, and understand their perspective.

Listening validates and shows respect; it is a form of affirmation. When we listen, we validate their existence. We say, "Your story matters." Respect is a way of honouring their journey, struggles, and triumphs. Listening fosters understanding and compassion, revealing nuances, fears, and hopes while helping us grasp their worldview. Compassionate listening fosters compassion, softening hearts and building bridges.

The act of listening holds the potential to foster understanding, strengthen connections, and improve overall relationships. So, let us remember the power of lending an ear and the positive impact it can have on the lives of those around us.

Listen and pay attention. Evangelism is not just waiting for an opportunity to speak; it needs to be a genuine conversation and exchange of ideas. When you ask questions like, "Are you happy in your life?" or "Do you ever feel as if you are missing out on something?" truly listen to the answers. Aside from making them feel that they have a willing listener, pay attention to what they are saying to respond accurately and convincingly. Take note of their body language as they speak.

We see Jesus doing this; we need to follow His example. He listened to people as they shared how they got to the places in life where they were, demonstrating compassion and empathy for their situations. He asked questions to ensure they understood things.

One such occasion for me was at a bus stop when a young lady approached. At first, I hesitated to initiate a conversation, but after a few minutes of waiting for the delayed bus, I opened with, "There is never a bus when you need one." She responded, expressing that she needed to get to her appointment. Her worry about the appointment added stress she didn't need. I could hear the anxiety in her voice, especially since she was attending alone.

As we discussed the importance of being on time, I listened to her struggles and asked if I could share my experience of coping with anxiety surrounding health appointments. I shared my personal testimony of how Jesus rescued me, and His promises to me, reassuring her that He could do the same for her. I then asked if she would like me to pray with her. She accepted my offer, and welcomed Jesus into her life.

"Do not be anxious about anything, but in everything by prayer and supplication with thanksgiving let your requests be made known to God. And the peace of God, which surpasses all understanding, will guard your hearts and your minds in Christ Jesus." (Philippians 4:6-7 NIV)

We must follow the same example:

- It facilitates clearer communication by minimising confusion, enhancing comprehension, and encouraging thoughtful responses.
- It is a crucial aspect of communication if you fail to understand the message being conveyed, you will also struggle to provide a substantial and meaningful response.
- It enhances your understanding and makes you a better communicator.
- It is one of the essential soft skills that indicate a person's ability to receive and interpret information in the communication process.
- It helps you understand your audience, allowing you to tailor your message to their needs and concerns.

Listening Techniques

1. **Active Listening**: Fully engage in the conversation by giving your undivided attention. Maintain eye contact, nod, and provide verbal cues to show that you are actively listening.
2. **Empathetic Listening:** Put yourself in the speaker's shoes. Strive to understand their feelings, emotions, and perspectives. Show empathy and validate their experiences.

3. **Reflective Listening**: Summarise what the speaker has said to ensure you have understood correctly. Use phrases like, "What I hear you saying is…" or "Let me make sure I understand…".
4. **Avoid Interrupting**: Allow the speaker to express their thoughts without interruption. Wait for natural pauses before responding.
5. **Ask Clarifying Questions**: If something is unclear, ask questions to seek clarification. Avoid making assumptions.
6. **Paraphrasing:** Restate the speaker's message in your own words. This demonstrates understanding and encourages further dialogue.
7. **Non-verbal Listening:** Pay attention to body language, facial expressions, and tone of voice. These cues provide additional context beyond words.
8. **Mindful Listening:** Be present in the moment. Avoid distractions and focus solely on the conversation. Keep your mobile phone on vibrate or silent.

Remember, effective listening is not just about hearing words; it is about understanding, connecting, and building stronger relationships. Once they have finished, you can summarise by saying, "From what you have said, this is what I understand you are experiencing…"

Effective listening is crucial for meaningful communication, but various barriers can hinder our ability to truly understand and connect with others. Let us explore some common barriers:

1. **Physical Barriers:**
    a. Noise: External sounds, such as construction noise, passing vehicles, or loud conversations, can interfere with hearing what is being said.
    b. Obstructions: People standing in your line of sight or sitting between you and the speaker can hinder effective listening.

c. Proximity: Stand as close as possible to the speaker without invading their personal space to listen clearly without distractions.
   d. Distance: Being too far from the speaker or having a poor phone connection can make it difficult to hear.
   e. Mobile Phones: Notifications from mobile phones can disrupt your focus while listening to the speaker.
   f. Interruptions: Frequent interruptions disrupt the flow of communication and hinder understanding.

2. Emotional Barriers:

   o Positive and Negative Emotions: Emotions such as excitement, anger, distraction, or upset feelings can disrupt concentration. For example, being upset about something earlier in the day might affect your focus during a conversation.

I have created a template that you can use to start writing your story for evangelism:

Fill in the Blanks:

- Before Christ came into my life: _____ (Describe what type of person you were and what your behaviour was like.) For example, "I was angry at the world and everyone I met. I would often get into physical fights and trouble, including time in prison."
- How did you come to know Christ? What were the circumstances? For example, "I went to a gospel concert with a friend and heard about the peace that comes from knowing God," or "I was listening to a gospel sermon, and it made me feel special.
- I came to believe in Christ: _____ (For instance, "through a friend who gave me a tract.

- After I came to believe in Christ what happened? "I am no longer angry at people or struggling to control my temper. I have learned to trust in God." (Proverbs 3:5-6).
- I have experienced the peace of God, and you can too.
- This story will take under five minutes to share the gospel.
- When people are asked to share their story, it should point to what God is doing in our lives.
- Sharing your story is about giving people insight into the narrative of our lives.

DOES and DONT'S:
DOES:
- How an individual came to realise their need for God.
- How they came to place their faith in God.
- What actions they took and how they felt.
- What insights they gained.
- What series of events led them to their current situation.

DON'T
- People often deliver lengthy speeches about their lives, yet they say very little about their lifestyles and what God has done.
- While it's important to preach or teach biblical doctrine, evangelism must also be rooted in that doctrine; it centers on what God has done.

Task the answer to the following questions:
1. What in your life is God doing now?
2. What has changed?
3. What is changing?
4. How are you experiencing God now?
   Leading Someone to God, Dialogue:

In this instance, I will demonstrate how to guide someone in accepting Christ as their Savior. You may have gone through John 3:16 or used the 3-circle technique with the unsaved. Do you believe that Jesus can forgive you of your sins?

Witness or Soul-Winner: Yes, I am unsaved.

You have just read how God says you can be born again.

Soul Winner: Do you admit that you are a sinner and need to repent?

Sinner: I have done some bad things; I don't think God will forgive me.

Soul Winner: God loves you so much. He sent His Son to pay the price for all the wrongs you have committed, so you don't have to feel guilty anymore. All God asks of you is to ask Him to forgive you and accept His Son as your Saviour.

He wants you to change your mind about repentance based on who God is.

He gave His Son to die for you, for me, and for the whole world. Anyone who believes in Christ or depends on Him for forgiveness and salvation will not perish, will not go to hell or Sheol, and will have eternal life.

If the sinner says yes at this point, you can invite them to pray. Ask if they would like to pray. The person may have never prayed before, so as the soul winner, you pray first. If the person is willing to pray, then let us pray. I will pray first and ask Jesus to forgive you and save you now. After that, you can repeat the prayer as I guide you in what to say.

Keep prayer short and simple!
SINNERS PRAYER:

- Lord, I confess that I am a sinner who needs saving
- Thank you, Jesus, for dying on the cross for me.
- I know I am a sinner. Forgive me and wash me with your blood.
- I want you to be the Lord of my life, I give you, my heart. Amen!

Once the person has finished praying, I suggest demonstrating an open acknowledgment of their decision. I would say: "Now you have asked Jesus to forgive you and come into your life. He promises to do so. Will you take my hand and shake as a sign between you and Christ of your decision to accept Jesus as your personal Saviour and give Him your heart? Will you do that?

If the sinner has been honest thus far, they will shake your hand as an open confession of their faith. If you are with a partner, I suggest they shake hands as well.

At this point, you can share a small Bible New Testament for the person to read, provide church contact details, and obtain their information, as this is where the genuine work begins.

Share John 3:18a KJV: "He that believeth on him is not condemned." John 3:36 He that believeth hath everlasting life.

You can ask the person another question at this point: "Have you trusted Christ or believe in Jesus?" The person will likely respond "yes." You can then say: "The way to know you are saved is not because you may feel different, but because the Bible says that when you trust and believe in Jesus, you have everlasting life."

Encourage the new convert to read the Scriptures, possibly starting with the book of John or Romans. Agree to meet with the new convert, be prepared to answer any questions, and guide them through the process of salvation.

Key Point: It is important to follow up with the new convert after their public confession of faith, focusing on reading the Bible, attending church, baptism, and church membership. We will discuss discipleship in a later chapter.

Chapter summary/Key takeaways

1. **It is important to practice sharing your story:**
   - Share with Enthusiasm: Convey your story with passion and reliance on the Holy Spirit. Speak clearly and in a relaxed manner, using a natural tone and volume.
   - Stick to Your Time Limit: Be concise and avoid overwhelming your listeners.

2. **Remember the Gospel:**
   - Christ-Centred: Always point to Jesus and His work on the cross.
   - Make Him Known: Clearly communicate the gospel message.

3. **Pray and Prepare Yourself:**
   - Courage: Evangelism can be intimidating, but rely on God's strength.
   - Support Group: Consider evangelizing with others for encouragement and advice.

4. **Never Ignore Boundaries:**
   - Respect people's boundaries. Choose appropriate locations and times for evangelism. Avoid contentious places or situations. Be courteous and sensitive to others' comfort levels.

5. **Not Listening Actively:**
   - Effective evangelism involves listening. Show empathy and understanding. Validate their feelings. Active listening builds trust and opens hearts to the Gospel.

6. **Being Silent:**
   - The most significant mistake is not sharing your faith. Fear of making mistakes or not having all the answers should not keep you silent.

By being a better listener, you can be a light in this world of self-absorption. People crave to be listened to, from the joys and struggles of their day to their deepest fears and most beautiful dreams. So, make a difference today—whether you are at the grocery store, heading to church, or spending time with your family. Go in God's power and step out in obedience. Your role is to sow seeds faithfully.

Give it a whirl and ask a great question today!

The Soul-winner's Toolbox

Here's a simple example of a flowchart for leading someone to Christ:

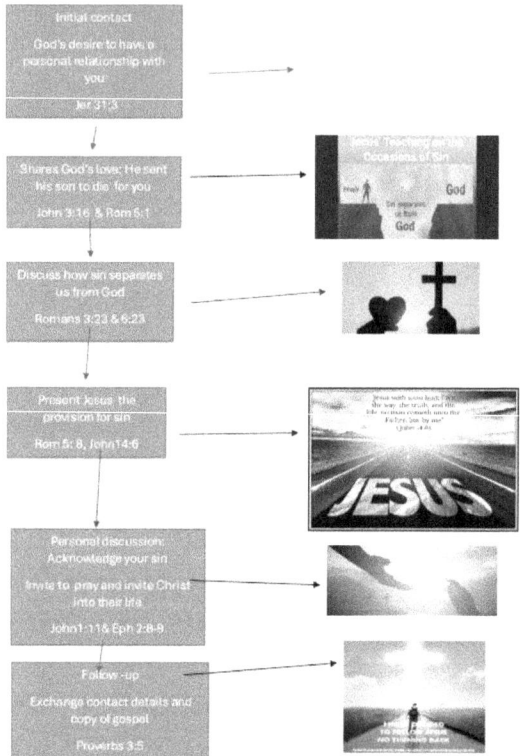

In the next chapter you will learn how to communicate creatively that will change people's heart.

Reflection:

Who did you share your testimony or the gospel with this week?

_____
_____
_____
_____
_____

Who do you want to share the gospel with this week?

_____
_____
_____
_____
_____
_____

Have you trained anyone in the gospel tool of sharing your testimony?

_____
_____
_____

_____
_____

Who will you encourage in sharing your story?
_____
_____
_____
_____
_____
_____

CHAPTER FOUR:
CRAFTING CONVERSATIONS BEYOND WORDS:

Crafting conversations beyond words is an art that transcends language and touches the depths of the soul. As soul winners, we communicate love, hope, and faith through actions, gestures, and our presence. This art involves reaching people's hearts through empathy and creative approaches.

Here are some ways to create meaningful connections beyond mere words:

The Warm Smile: A smile is a universal language; it says, "You matter." Greet people with genuine warmth, and let your eyes convey kindness.

Act of Kindness: A smile is a universal language; it says, "You matter." Greet people with genuine warmth and let your eyes convey kindness.

Hold the door for someone, help carry groceries, or offer your seat on public transport. Volunteer at a shelter, clean up a neighbourhood park, or visit the sick. Actions demonstrate love more profoundly than words; these small acts speak volumes.

Listening Intently: Sometimes, the most powerful conversations happen in silence. Be fully present when someone shares their heart, and listen without interrupting or judging.

Touch and Comfort: A gentle touch on the shoulder or a reassuring hug can convey empathy and compassion. Be sensitive to cultural norms, but don't underestimate the power of physical connection.

Prayerful Presence: Sit with someone in their pain. Pray silently for them and let your spirit intercede on their behalf.

Shared Meals: Invite someone for a meal; breaking bread together fosters fellowship and opens hearts.

Eye Contact: Focus on the person. This communicates respect, sincerity, and acknowledgment of their humanity.

Celebrate Milestones: Attend birthdays, graduations, and weddings. Your presence says, "I rejoice with you."

Forgiveness and Reconciliation: Sometimes, actions speak louder than apologies. Extend forgiveness, seek reconciliation, and mend broken relationships.

Model Christlikeness: Live out the Gospel. Let your life be a testimony. When people see your integrity, they will want to know the Source.

Acts of Generosity: Give sacrificially; whether it is your time, resources, or talents, generosity reflects God's heart.

Remember, our lives are the canvas upon which the Gospel is painted. Let your actions be brushstrokes of love, pointing others to the Saviour.

Crafting communication beyond words, here are practical ways to go beyond verbal communication:

Prayer Walks and Prayer: Pray silently as you walk through your community, interceding for people, schools, businesses, and local needs.

Ask for Prayer Requests: Engage with strangers and offer to pray for them. Carry a notebook to make notes of what you observe, pray about, and the people you pray with. When possible, take contact details so you can follow up.

Storytelling through Art or Music:

Art Shows: Showcase Christian art that tells a redemptive story.

Music Events: Host concerts or worship nights where lyrics convey the Gospel.

Living a Transformed Life: Model Christ by letting your actions reflect your faith. Live out love, forgiveness, and integrity.

Invite Curiosity: When people see a changed life, they will ask questions; be ready to share your story.

Remember, communication extends beyond words. Our lives become living testimonies, drawing others to the One who transforms hearts.

The Evangelist's Compass:

"The Evangelist's Compass serves as a crucial guide for those passionate about effective evangelism. We explore the essential tools every soul winner needs. From prayer to understanding the Gospel message, we set our bearings for the journey ahead.

Let's examine what this entails:

The Evangelist's Compass-Navigating the Spiritual Landscape

As an evangelist, you are called to be a spiritual navigator, a guide who points lost souls toward the eternal truth. Just as a compass directs a traveller through uncharted territories, your role is to lead others to the life-transforming message of Jesus Christ.

1. True North: The Gospel Message

Your compass needle always points to the Gospel—the heart of evangelism. Understand it deeply, articulate it clearly, and share it boldly. Memorise key Scriptures that encapsulate the Good News, and let them guide your conversations.

2. East: The Urgency of Salvation

The sun rises in the east, signalling a new day. Similarly, urgency drives your mission. Recognise that every soul matters. Time is fleeting, and eternity hangs in the balance.

3. West: The Setting Sun of Lost Opportunities

The west symbolises the end of the day. Lost opportunities fade like twilight. Do not delay. Share the Gospel today; tomorrow may be too late.

4. South: Compassion and Empathy

The south represents warmth and compassion. Approach others with empathy. Listen to their stories, understand their pain, and offer them hope.

5. North: The Holy Spirit's Leading

The North Star guides travellers; likewise, the Holy Spirit directs your steps.

Pray for sensitivity to His promptings, for He knows where hearts are ready.

6. The Full Circle: Discipleship

A compass completes its circle, just as evangelism leads to discipleship. Walk alongside new believers, nurture their growth, and equip them to become soul winners too. May "The Evangelist's Compass" empower you to navigate the spiritual terrain, leading lost souls toward the eternal sunrise of salvation.

Choose an appropriate location and time to share your message with as many receptive people as possible. High-traffic areas that are good for evangelism might include business districts, street fairs, municipal markets, and college campuses. Avoid evangelising around churches of other faiths and places that might be contentious or difficult. For example, a train station platform at 8 AM may not find most people in a chatting mood. Use your judgment: it might be a great idea to evangelise outside a nightclub on a Friday night, but it could also lead to arguments.

Some of my best evangelism takes place in the park, where people are often more relaxed and willing to listen. I can recall numerous times I have gone to the park and engaged in deep, meaningful conversations with strangers that led them to accept salvation.

One such occasion was during the summer months when the weather was beautiful in London. I visited a park close to my local church. Upon entering I assessed the people present and noticed a group of around six people sitting on the grass, two ladies chatting, and a young lady by herself. I was drawn to the young woman alone. I indicated to my evangelising partner that we could speak with her.

We greeted her, and my partner started the conversation by asking about her pet dog. The discussion swiftly moved to introductions and the reason for our visit. The young lady shared her name, which by coincidence was the same as mine. After a while, we asked if there was anything she would like us to pray about. She revealed that her mother had recently passed away, and she was missing her dearly.

I encouraged her by sharing my own story of the death of my parents and the strategies I have used to cope. We discussed the afterlife and the significance of Christ's death. She acknowledged that she had not been attending church or reading her Bible as much as she should. I explained that having Jesus as her personal Saviour was the only guarantee of spending eternity with God. We prayed with her, provided information about salvation and accepting Christ, along with our church details. We left her smiling and grateful to have met us.

This experience reaffirmed my belief that God guides and directs our paths. The Holy Spirit led us to this young woman who needed to hear the Gospel of Salvation; she needed to hear the truth and seek God's direction for her life (Isaiah 61:1-3).

On another occasion in the park, I spoke with a young lady about salvation. By the end, she was happy to receive more information about Jesus and how to become saved. I was able to guide her toward attending a church in her neighbourhood.

Another time I met two young men in the park and was able to share the Gospel with them. Initially, one of the young men was not keen to listen; his body language appeared defensive. The other young man explained that he had once been a regular church attendee but had stopped going for a while. After exploring deeper, I understood why the other young man was so defensive. After a few minutes I gained their trust and was able to witness to both.

I have found that going to the park and interacting with people is a positive experience, as they are more receptive and respond more easily to the Gospel.

Creative ways to Evangelize Effectively

Effective evangelism involves creativity, authenticity, and a heart for people. It's not just about words, it's about living out Christ's love. Sharing the Gospel without words can be a powerful way to demonstrate this love and make an impact. Here are some creative ways to evangelise without verbal communication:

Be creative, genuine, and intentional in your actions!

Nicole Bennett Blake

Here are some creative ways to share the Gospel:

USING PICTORIAL TO ENGAGE PEOPLE: what do man see VS How Jesus sees

Man: Children sit with an adult, while Jesus imparts wisdom; "Train up a child in the way he should go."

Man: People ascend the escalator, a child gazes wistfully; Jesus consoles, "Cast your cares upon the Lord."

Man: Family packs the car for a trip, whereas Jesus promises, "Wherever you go, I will be with you."

Man: Boy rests in his seat within the car; Jesus observes, "Rest in the Lord and His word."

Children engage in a race, yet Jesus encourages, "You have run the race, press towards the mark."

Use pictures to engage people by asking them what they observe. You can then explain how Jesus sees us with compassion and love from a Father's perspective.

Thanks to my beautiful sister Amy Rose, who introduced me to the survival kit gift bag and its resources. I have incorporated her survival kit gift bag to illustrate its symbolism and how to use it. By Maxine Abrams

Items Included and Their Reminder	
Toothpick: to pick out the good qualities in others (Matt 7: 1)	
1. Rubber band: to be flexible; things may not always go the way you want, but it will work out (Romans 8:28)	
2. Band aid: to remind you to heal hurt feelings, yours or someone else's (Col 3: 12-14)	
3. Pencil: to remind you to list your blessings every day (Eph 1:3)	Perhaps you know someone who would appreciate a goodie bag filled with these items, along with a note explaining what they symbolise
4. Eraser: to remind you that everyone makes mistakes (sin), and it's OK (Gen 50:16-21)	
5. Chewing gum: stick with it, and you can accomplish anything with Jesus (Phil 4:13)	
6. Mint: you are worth a mint to your heavenly Father (John 3:16-17)	
7. Hershey kiss: everyone needs a kiss or hug every day (1 John 4:7)	
8. Tea bag: to relax daily and go over that list of God's blessings (1 Thess 5:18).	

Other ways you can engage your neighbourhood using the Gift Bag:

Incorporating a gift bag can be a thoughtful and impactful way to enhance your message. Here's how to effectively use a gift bag and the items you can include as part of your soul-winning efforts:

1. **Symbolism and Purpose:**
   - Intention: Explain to your readers that the gift bag symbolises God's love and grace. Just as a gift is freely given, so is salvation through Jesus Christ.
   - Contents: Fill the gift bag with items that represent spiritual truths. For example:
     1. **Bible:** Include a small New Testament or a pocket-sized Bible.
     2. **Cross:** Add a small wooden or metal cross as a reminder of Christ's sacrifice.
     3. **Prayer Card:** Include a card with a simple prayer or an encouraging Bible verse.
     4. **Candy:** Use individually wrapped candies (like mints) to represent the sweetness of God's love.
     5. **Tract:** Slip in a gospel tract or a brief explanation of salvation.
     6. **Personal Touch:** Consider adding a handwritten note or a bookmark with your contact information.

2. **Presentation:**
   - **Warm Introduction:** Begin with a friendly greeting as you share the gift bag. Let them know you've brought a small gift to share.

- **Conversation Starter:** Use the gift bag as an icebreaker. Ask if they've ever considered their spiritual journey or if they have questions about faith.
- **Share the Message:** Briefly explain the significance of each item as you present it.
  - For example:
    1. "This Bible represents God's Word, which guides us."
    2. "The cross reminds us of Jesus' sacrifice for our sins."
    3. "Would you like to pray together?"

Invite Further Discussion: Offer to talk more about faith, answer questions, or pray with them.

Natural Opportunities: Look for times when sharing the gift bag feels natural, like during a visit, outreach event, or a chance encounter.

Sensitive Approach: Be mindful of their receptivity. If they decline respect their decision graciously.

Digital Prize Wheel for Outreach Events:

When it comes to evangelism, creative tools can be highly effective in engaging people and sharing the message of Christ. Here are some ideas for using spinning wheels:

- Consider incorporating a digital prize wheel at outreach events or gatherings.
- Participants can spin the virtual wheel, landing on a prize or prompt related to evangelism.

Remember, the goal is to compassionately care for those who do not yet know Jesus and to share the gospel courageously. May your efforts bear the fruit of the Holy Spirit as you spin the wheel of evangelism!

Here are a few more creative tools and approaches for evangelism:

1. **Prayer Walks**
   - Organize a Prayer Walk: Plan a group or individual prayer walk in your community.
   - As you walk, pray for the people, businesses, schools, and other aspects of the neighbourhood. Be open to conversations with anyone you meet, offering to pray for their needs.
   - Consider leaving small notes with encouraging Bible verses in public spaces (e.g., park benches, bus stops) for people to find. Make prayer walks a regular practice so that people come to recognise your presence.

Gospel Tracts with a Twist:
   - Design unique gospel tracts that stand out.
   - Create bookmarks, stickers, or small cards with engaging visuals and concise gospel messages.
   - Distribute these at events, coffee shops, libraries, or other public spaces.
   - Include a QR code that links to an online resource, your church's service and prayer line or a video explaining the gospel in more detail.

Interactive Art or Chalkboard Evangelism:
   - Set up an interactive art station or chalkboard in a public area.
   - Invite passersby to contribute to a collaborative art piece or write their thoughts, prayers, or questions.

- Use this as an opportunity to engage in conversations about faith and share the gospel.

Storytelling Nights:

- Host storytelling events where people can share personal stories of faith, redemption, or transformation.
- Encourage attendees to share how they encountered Jesus or experienced His love.
- Stories have a powerful impact, resonating deeply with listeners.

Blessing Bags:

- Assemble small care packages with essentials like snacks, hygiene items, and a gospel tract.
- Keep them in your car or backpack to give to homeless individuals or others in need.
- Include a note expressing God's love and an invitation to connect with a local church.

Digital Evangelism:

- Use social media, blogs, or podcasts to share your faith.
- Create short videos, infographics, or written content addressing common questions about Christianity.
- Engage with people online, answering questions and pointing them to Jesus.

Remember, creativity in evangelism opens doors to reach people in diverse ways. Pray for guidance, remain sensitive to the Holy Spirit, and step out in faith as you share the good news.

The gift bag serves as a tool, a tangible expression of God's love. But the true impact lies in the conversation and the chance to share the gospel.

Here's an example of how I've creatively shared the gospel:

Once, I visited my local supermarket, bought bottles of water, and received permission to hand them out with church information to people as they left. I also use gift bags and food parcels to connect with people in my community. For instance, during Christmas, I distribute food parcels to shut-ins and others in need, including information about local churches and invitations to special services.

PRACTICAL TIPS:

Here are some creative ways to use technology for evangelism:

1. Podcasting

- Start a Podcast: Share faith-based content, interviews, and discussions. Podcasts can reach listeners during commutes, workouts, or leisure time.

2. Social Media Outreach

- Active Social Media Accounts: Use platforms like Facebook, Instagram, X (Twitter), and TikTok to share sermon snippets, inspirational quotes, and live prayer sessions.
- Engaging Content: Create interactive posts, polls, and Q&A sessions to connect with your audience.

3. YouTube Channel

- **Video Content:** Upload sermons, Bible studies, and testimonies. Create short, engaging videos addressing common questions about faith.
- **Live Streaming:** Stream church services, special events, and live Q&A sessions to reach a broader audience.

4. Blogging

- **Write a Blog:** Share articles addressing spiritual questions, offering encouragement, and providing insights on Christian living.

- **SEO Optimization:** Use keywords and SEO techniques to reach people searching for answers online.

5. Email Campaigns

- **Newsletters:** Send regular updates, devotionals, and event invitations to your congregation and interested individuals.
- **Personalized Messages:** Tailor messages to different audience segments to enhance relevance and engagement.

6. Responsive Website

- **User-Friendly Design:** Ensure your church's website is easy to navigate and mobile-friendly. Include sermon archives, event calendars, and contact information.
- **Online Giving:** Provide options for online donations and tithing.

7. Mobile Apps

- Church App: Develop an app with features like sermon streaming, event notifications, and Bible study tools.
- Push Notifications: Send reminders and inspirational messages directly to users' phones.

8. Virtual Reality (VR)

- VR Church Services: Create immersive virtual reality experiences for church services and Bible studies.
- Virtual Tours: Offer virtual tours of your church and its activities to attract new visitors.

9. Interactive Online Events

- Webinars and Workshops: Host online events covering topics related to faith and Christian living.

- Virtual Small Groups: Facilitate small group meetings and Bible studies through video conferencing platforms like Zoom.

10. Digital Evangelism Teams

- Online Missionaries: Train and equip a team to engage in digital evangelism on social media, forums, and online communities.
- Social Listening: Monitor online conversations to identify opportunities for sharing the Gospel and offering support.

ENCOURAGEMENT:

1. Feed My Sheep: Following Jesus's example, consider feeding those in need. Volunteer with hunger-relief ministries, donate to food banks, or buy a meal for someone. Acts of kindness reveal Christ's love.
2. Speak to the Spirit of a Person: Rather than warning people about condemnation, speak God's Word to their spirit. Scripture has power and won't return empty (Hebrews 4:12). Share verses and trust God's Word to work within them.
3. Just Talk – Don't Debate: Avoid theological debates. Our role is to share God's Word, not argue. Instead, focus on delivering the truth in love (Philippians 2:14-15).

   - **Choose the Right Environment:** Community Service: Show God's love through acts of kindness. Serve others and let your actions speak.
   - **Personal Testimonies:** Share your journey of faith; personal stories resonate deeply.
   - **Creative Events: Movie Nights:** Host a faith-based film night and discuss its themes afterward.
   - **Art or Music Shows:** Showcase Christian art or music to spark meaningful conversations.

Social Media Evangelism

   - **Create Shareable Content:** Post Bible verses, testimonies, and thoughtful questions.
   - **Engage in Conversations:** Respond to comments and messages with grace and truth.

Random Acts of Kindness

   - **Pay for Someone's Coffee:** Surprise a stranger by covering their coffee or meal.

- **Leave Encouraging Notes:** Place uplifting notes in public spaces for people to find.

Remember, **authenticity** matters. Be genuine, listen well, and let the Holy Spirit guide your conversations.

Crafting communication beyond words

This involves more than just the content of your message and how you deliver it. Let us delve into this concept:

- Message and Delivery
  - Message: This refers to the verbal part of communication—the words you speak or write.
  - Delivery: The non-verbal elements include all the ways you express yourself beyond words. This can be divided into visual and vocal cues:
    - Visual cues: Your appearance, presence, body language, posture, gestures, facial expressions, and eye contact.
    - Vocal cues: The tone of voice, volume, and pitch you use.
- Self-Awareness
  - The first step toward greater influence is self-awareness.
  - Recognize where your message and delivery align or diverge.
  - Be mindful of what your body language, facial expressions, eye contact, physical mannerisms, and vocal tone communicate.
- Influence Beyond Words
  - Authentic Connection: Influential communicators build genuine connections with listeners and readers.

- Engagement: They focus on engaging with their audience rather than solely on notes or slides.
- Purposeful Gestures: Their gestures add to the message rather than distracting from it.
- Remember, effective communication goes beyond crafting a strong message and honing delivery skills it's about connecting authentically and engaging beyond mere words.

The Power of Five:

The Five Finger Method is a simple and memorable way to share the Gospel. This method is easy to learn and hard to forget, making it a powerful tool for communicating the Good News. Using the five fingers on your hand, it guides you through key points of the Gospel. Here's how it works:

1. **Thumb – Jesus' Birth:** Jesus was born in Bethlehem over 2,000 years ago, fulfilling Old Testament prophecies of the Messiah's birth through a virgin.
2. **Index Finger – Jesus' Life:** Jesus lived a sinless life, teaching us how to love and serve others through His miracles and parables.
3. **Middle Finger – Jesus' Death:** Jesus died on the cross, paying the penalty for our sins. His sacrifice grants us forgiveness and reconciliation with God.
4. **Ring Finger – Our Response:** We must respond personally to Jesus' invitation by repenting of our sins and placing our faith in Him.
5. **Little Finger – Eternal Life:** Through faith in Jesus, we receive the gift of eternal life and a restored relationship with God.

Another great tool is the "Evangecube".

I had the pleasure of working with a team from the International Commission Organisation that came to the United Kingdom. During this time, I was introduced to the EvangeCube and witnessed firsthand the effectiveness of this small but powerful tool for sharing the Gospel.

The EvangeCube is a unique evangelism tool designed to visually present the Gospel of Jesus Christ. It consists of eight smaller blocks connected in a way that allows it to unfold and reveal seven different images. These images illustrate key aspects of the Christian message:

The EvangeCube is simple and clearly conveys the Gospel of Jesus Christ. It is a tool that can be used by everyone, including parents, missionaries, and more. Its portability makes it easy to carry and demonstrate the Gospel, making it ideal for church outreach, Sunday school classes, conversation starters, and day to day evangelism. It is a powerful resource for sharing the Gospel and leading others to Jesus.

Separation from God: The first image shows the separation between humanity and God due to sin.

Christ's Sacrifice: The following images depict Jesus' crucifixion, burial, and resurrection.

Salvation: It then reveals the open tomb, symbolizing Jesus' victory over death.

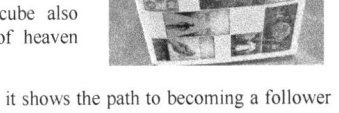

Heaven and Hell: The cube also illustrates the concepts of heaven and hell.

Following Christ: Finally, it shows the path to becoming a follower of Christ.

The EvangeCube is highly portable and can be used in any language, making it a popular tool for mission trips and church outreach events.

May this book inspire many soul-winners to use creative methods like this to reach hearts for Christ!

Chapter summary/Key takeaways

Remember, starting a conversation about faith can be both meaningful and impactful. Here are some gentle and effective ways to initiate such discussions:

Ask Open-Ended Questions: Start by posing open-ended questions that encourage reflection and sharing. For example:

- "What role does spirituality play in your life?"
- "Have you ever contemplated the deeper questions of existence?"
- "What do you believe happens after we die?"

These questions invite personal insights and pave the way for deeper conversations.

Share Your Own Journey: Authenticity is powerful. Share your own faith journey, struggles, and moments of growth. For instance:

- "I have found a great deal of hope and purpose through my faith. How about you?"
- "I used to have doubts too, but exploring my beliefs has been transformative."

Vulnerability often encourages others to open up their hearts as well.

Use Current Events or Life Experiences:

o Relate faith to everyday life. Discuss how faith intersects with current events, personal experiences, or challenges.
o For example: "Given everything happening in the world, I've been reflecting on faith and hope."

"I recently read a book that challenged my beliefs. Have you ever had a similar experience?"

Teach **Others** to **Do** the **Same:**

Teach your friends how to evangelise too and do it together! Saint Paul writes, "What you have heard from me…entrust to faithful people who will be able to teach others as well" (2 Timothy 2:2). Jesus sent His apostles into the world by reaching out to individuals who could teach others.

You can fulfill the call to evangelise by developing deep friendships, inviting people to follow Jesus, and teaching others to do the same!

The hardest part of evangelism is starting. We often do anything but begin. We read books on evangelism, soul winning, and even pray about it. We attend training sessions, but if you haven't started yet, now is the time. The best way to learn is through action; none of us is particularly skilled at first. We all need to learn through practical repetition and consistency.

Dear Fellow Soul Winners,

As we turn the page to the next chapter of "The Soul Winners Toolbox," we enter a realm of profound impact: the art of discipling the disciple. Here, we delve beyond mere evangelism; we become spiritual mentors, guiding others toward a deeper walk with Jesus.

Reflection:

1. What steps can you take to grow in your confidence as a soul-winner?

_____
_____
_____
_____
_____
_____

2. What motivates you to share the Gospel with others?

_____
_____
_____
_____
_____
_____

3. How do you handle rejection or indifference when sharing the Gospel?

_____
_____
_____
_____
_____
_____

4. How do you rely on the Holy Spirit's guidance during evangelism?

_____
_____
_____
_____
_____
_____

CHAPTER FIVE:
DISCIPLING THE DISCIPLE – UNLEASHING THE SOUL WINNER WITHIN

Evangelism is about following up, teaching and building relationships, we are all called to participate. Discipleship is rooted in a journey of faith, guiding new believers as they grow spiritually. But how do you respond when someone has just accepted Christ? The answer is "follow-up" — a crucial process of nurturing and cultivating the faith of a new believer.

This journey requires your support and encouragement. Be patient, loving, and available to answer any questions they may have. Follow-up refers to the intentional and ongoing discipleship provided to those who have recently accepted Jesus Christ as their Lord and Saviour. It is not a one-time event but a continual effort to nurture their faith, foster spiritual growth, and integrate them into the Christian community. Your care plays a vital role in helping new converts establish a strong foundation in their faith, guiding them in understanding their new relationship with God and learning how to grow and share their faith.

Reach out to the new believer within 24–48 hours, as the first day is critical in establishing their walk with the Lord. Arrange to meet and discuss how their new faith becomes part of their daily life. Be available for the Holy Spirit to work through you as you affirm the new relationship and set up a follow-up meeting. Satan may attempt to sow doubt or discouragement, so your presence and willingness to talk can be a valuable source of support.

What should you discuss in your first follow-up meeting? The purpose is to build a personal connection, help the new Christian understand the assurance of salvation, and introduce them to God's love.

Personalise your time. Personalize your time by asking meaningful questions; don't focus on yourself, but instead, listen and talk about their interests or common ground you share.

Building a strong spiritual foundation for new converts is essential for their growth and stability in faith. Use your time together to discuss spiritual growth and foundational truths they need to know, such as:

- Assurance of salvation (Hebrews 13:5; 1 John 1:9)
- Knowledge of Jesus Christ (John 20:31; Romans 10:17)
- Forgiveness and confession of sins (Romans 5:6-9; 1 John 1:9)
- The ministry of the Holy Spirit in their life (John 14:25-26; Ephesians 5:18)
- Their new identity in Christ (2 Corinthians 5:17)

During this time, new believers can start growing in maturity and become multiplying disciples. Christians are called to help others come to Christ and support them as they grow in their new faith.

The Call to Multiply & The Joy of Multiplication:

The greatest joy is seeing new soul winners emerge. I can still remember the very first time I led someone to accepting Christ—the joy I felt was incomparable to anything I have ever felt.

As we explore mentoring, training, and releasing others into the harvest, we learn it's never too early to encourage new believers to share their testimonies. When they talk to others about how God has changed their lives, it both solidifies their faith and demonstrates God's work in action. Take them along when you share your faith, training them in how to share the gospel. This enables them to become multiplying disciples, watching God touch others' lives just as He touched theirs. Encourage them to share both struggles and victories with a trusted mentor or friend.

The Holy Spirit's role is essential in this journey. Help new believers understand who the Holy Spirit is and what it means to walk in the Spirit's power, not their own. If we try to live the Christian life through our own strength alone, we will surely fall away. "Not by might nor by power, but by My Spirit: Says the Lord of Hosts". Zechariah 4:6-9b. Allow God to be your strength. "I can do all things through him who strengthens me" (Philippians 4:13).

In follow-up, we play an important part, but ultimately God does the work. Don't be offended if people aren't interested. God is the one pursuing them, and He will bring about the fruit of salvation. He has promised in His Word to complete the good work He has begun in us. When new believers have questions and doubts, it's important to support and encourage them immediately. Offer a specific meeting time and make it easy for them to say "yes."

Imagine a blacksmith's forge, where raw iron transforms into a finely crafted blade. Similarly, discipleship Molds hearts, shaping them into vessels that carry the Gospel flame.

Our task is twofold:

1. Nurturing Growth: We water the seeds of faith planted during evangelism. We teach, correct, and encourage. We model Christlikeness, revealing the path of discipleship.

2. Multiplying Impact: Discipleship isn't a solo journey—it's a relay race. We pass the baton of faith, ensuring that each disciple becomes a soul winner too. Our goal is a chain reaction of transformed lives.

Nicole Bennett Blake

🔨 The Anvil of Relationship 🔨

Discipleship is not a curriculum; it is a relationship—an anvil where character hammers out purpose. Here is how we wield the hammer:

1. **Investment:** We invest time, love, and wisdom. We listen to their doubts, celebrate their victories, and walk alongside them.

2. **Modeling:** Our lives become living textbooks. We show them how to pray, study Scripture, and love unconditionally. Our scars become their roadmap.

3. **Challenge:** We stretch their faith muscles. We ask tough questions, provoke thought, and ignite hunger for God's Word.

🔑 The Toolbox Unveiled 🔑

Within this chapter lies a treasure trove of tools through which the Great Commission can come to fruition:

1. The Compass of Accountability: Teach them to navigate life's storms. Accountability partners keep them on course.

2. The Mirror of Self-Reflection: Encourage introspection. What areas need growth? What sins need repentance?

3. The Lantern of Prayer: Illuminate their path. Prayer is not a monologue; it is a dialogue with the Almighty.

4. The Whetstone of Scripture: Sharpen their spiritual sword. Daily Bible study keeps their edge keen.

5. The Forge of Community: Iron sharpens iron. Connect them with fellow believers.

🌳 The Sapling Becomes the Oak 🌳

As we disciple, we witness saplings grow into oaks. Their roots dig deep, their branches stretch toward heaven. And soon, they too scatter seeds of hope.

So, my fellow soul winner, let's embrace this sacred task. Let's disciple the disciple, knowing that eternity echoes our efforts. The Great Commission is not a solo mission—it is a relay. Pass the baton. Multiply the flame.

Onward, soul winner! The harvest awaits.

In His service,

Nicole Bennett Blake

P.S. Remember, both Heaven and Hell await the outcome of what you do with this chapter.

Eternity calls.

As stewards of this precious transformation, we step into the role of spiritual parents, nurturing and guiding these newborn believers in exploring the art of discipleship—the intentional process of shaping converts into committed disciples. From the initial encounter to lifelong growth, let us delve into practical strategies, pitfalls to avoid, and the joy of witnessing lives transformed by grace.

"go and make disciples of all nations..." matthew 28:19-20

Jesus last command or instruction to his disciples were to do four things.

1. They were to **"go."**
2. They were to **"make disciples"**; this meant they were to go and share their stories of Jesus, how He had impacted their lives.

3. They were to **"baptise."** Jesus gave them the authority to baptise new disciples as a way of initiating them into the faith.
4. They were to **"teach."** Up until this point, Jesus had not given them authority to teach; instead, He had given them authority to heal the sick, power over all devils, the ability to cure diseases, and the task of preaching the kingdom of God (Luke 9:1-2).

Jesus knew that He would not be around much longer, so He wanted the disciples to share all the teaching He had imparted to them. The pupils must now become the teachers. So, it is with us as Christians, we must disciple new converts so they can grow and learn to become teachers as they grow in faith.

If we do not make disciples to carry on the work of the Lord, we have not fulfilled the Great Commission.

UNDERSTANDING SALVATION STAGES:

Making Believers Accountable

Discipling new believers effectively is both a sacred privilege and a responsibility. As you walk alongside them, remember that the new convert will not reach spiritual maturity right away. Give them time to grow. As believers, we need to teach new converts that salvation unfolds in stages. Do not deliver a message of false hope; instead, deliver the true Gospel, the Gospel of the "Good News." Anyone who claims that becoming a Christian makes life always wonderful and perfect has clearly never read the New Testament.

The Soul-winner's Toolbox

> **C** - connect with others
> **O**- Obey the great commission
> **S**- Share the Gospel
> **T**- Train new believers

Justification is by faith in Christ alone, apart from works (Romans 3:28). It represents the initial act of being declared righteous before God. Sanctification is the ongoing process of growing into Christlikeness, which is an essential aspect of Christian growth. This involves daily transformation by the Holy Spirit (1 Thessalonians 4:3). Additionally, help them understand that glorification is the future completion of their salvation when they receive their resurrected bodies (1 Corinthians 15:51-53).

It is important for us to pray for new believers, trusting God to work in their lives. Praying with them shows that we care and provides them with an example of how to communicate with God. Paul prayed for his disciples, confident that God would complete the work He started in them. Throughout the Gospels, Jesus also prayed for His disciples. In 1 Thessalonians, Paul emphasizes the importance of praying for new believers.

He shared the Word of God with them, which is essential for new believers to learn how to read the Bible and listen to God through His Word. We know from experience that we grow in our faith by consistently studying the Bible and spending time with Him. God's Word is our spiritual food, and we cannot live without it.

Encourage new converts to read the Bible, starting with the Gospel of John. This will heighten their curiosity and ignite a hunger and thirst for the Word of God. Encourage them to keep a journal of what they have read, as well as any questions or thoughts that arise during their

> **C** - connect with others
> **O**- Obey the great commission
> **S**- Share the Gospel
> **T**- Train new believers

reading time. This practice can help them understand what they are reading.

We must also learn to share our lives with new believers, being open and honest about both the good and the bad, as well as what God is teaching us. Spend time together doing fun activities—go shopping, play video games, or have lunch. When you become someone's friend, you demonstrate who you are and show that being a Christian can be enjoyable. Let them see that you care about them and desire more than just to share spiritual things.

Paul likens himself to a spiritual parent to the new believers, saying, "But we proved to be gentle among you, as a nursing mother tenderly cares for her own children" (1 Thessalonians 2:7). We, too, can act as caring parents for new believers, watching over them, nurturing them, encouraging them, correcting them, and holding them accountable.

Introduce new believers to other Christians who can encourage and support them in this new phase of life. Invite them to join your Bible study or church. If you are meeting with them to go through follow-up materials, ask some of your Christian friends to join as well. This way, they can make new friends, hear different perspectives, and learn from others.

1. **Teach Holiness and Sin Awareness**:
   - Hate Sin: Help new believers recognise that all sin is spiritual poison. Encourage them to flee from sin and pursue holiness (1 Peter 1:15-16).
   - Repentance: Teach them the importance of repentance, turning away from sin and turning toward God. Encourage them to change their thought processes!

2. **Emphasise Prayer and Bible Study**:

- Prayer: Encourage regular communication with God. Teach them to bring every thought and concern to Him (Philippians 4:6).
- Bible Study: Show them how to read and study the Bible. Start with the Gospels or a simple devotional plan.

3. **Model a Vibrant Christian Life**:

    - Authenticity: Let them see your faith in action. Demonstrate prayer, worship, and obedience.
    - Involve Them: Invite them to church, small groups, and service opportunities.

4. **Provide Resources**:

    - Books and Devotionals: Recommend discipleship materials or devotionals.
    - Online Sermons and Podcasts: Point them to solid teaching resources.

5. **Encourage Fellowship and Community**:

    - **Connect Them:** Introduce them to other believers, as fellowship is crucial for growth.
    - **Accountability:** Remember that building a spiritual foundation takes time and intentional effort. Be patient, pray for them, and celebrate their progress.
    - **Scripture Verse:** Share a Bible verse with them.

- **Personal Testimony:** Encourage them to share their faith story.
- **Prayer Request:** Ask if there is anything they would like prayer for.
- **Invite a Friend:** Encourage them to invite someone to church.
- **Gospel Message:** Briefly share the good news of Jesus.

Chapter summary/Key takeaways

Repentance: Teach them that repentance involves turning away from sin and turning toward God. Encourage them to change their thought processes!

Start with Relationship:

- Build Trust: Invest time in getting to know them personally. Genuine care and friendship lay the foundation for effective discipleship.
- Be Available: Be accessible for questions, conversations, and prayer.

2. **Teach the Basics of Faith**:

- Foundational Truths: Cover essential doctrines: salvation, the Trinity, the Bible's authority, prayer, and the role of the Holy Spirit.
- Bible Reading: Teach them how to read and study the Bible. Start with the Gospel of John or a simple devotional plan.

3. **Model a Vibrant Christian Life**:

- Authenticity: Let them see your faith in action by demonstrating prayer, worship, and obedience.
- Involve Them: Invite them to church, small groups, and service opportunities.

4. **Encourage Spiritual Habits**:

- Prayer: Teach them how to pray both personally and corporately.

- Scripture Memorization: Help them hide God's Word in their hearts.
- Fellowship: Connect them with other believers.

5. **Address Common Questions and Challenges**:
   - Assurance of Salvation: Reassure them of God's grace.
   - Dealing with Doubts: Equip them to navigate spiritual struggles.
   - Overcoming Sin: Teach them about repentance and reliance on God's strength.

6. **Provide Resources**:
   - Books: Recommend discipleship materials and devotionals.
   - Online Sermons: Direct them to solid teaching.

7. **Pray Together**:
   - Pray Regularly: Intercede for their growth, challenges, and spiritual journey.
   - Model Prayer: Show them how to pray effectively.

Remember, taking care of a newborn is a lot of work! It *is a process*. A couple of things to remember: every young Christian will need to continue to learn from the Scriptures. We need to start at the beginning and build. Do not try to teach everything all at once! Follow-up is a process.

But if you have done your job well, by God's grace, your newborn friends will soon be walking, talking, and feeding themselves spiritually. They will be on their way to becoming mature disciples of Christ! Discipleship is a lifelong process. Be patient, loving, and committed. As you pour into new believers, you participate in God's redemptive work.

Finally, let me remind you once again of the challenge Jesus gave before He finished His earthly ministry and ascended to heaven in Matthew 28:19-20: "Therefore go and make disciples of all nations, baptising them in the name of the Father and of the Son and of the Holy Spirit and teaching them to obey everything I have commanded you, and surely I will be with you always, to the very end of the age." Jesus was speaking to His disciples. He had a great influence on them for over three years; it was now time for them to demonstrate first-hand instruction, teaching, and modeling Jesus' way of authenticity and compassion in soul winning.

In the challenge Jesus left, the disciples were to "go and make disciples of all nations." It's clear Jesus was saying this would happen as a result of the disciples actually going and getting into close proximity to the people they hoped to influence. By doing so, they would have opportunities to start conversations, build relationships, and influence the people they'd come to know.

Jesus also stressed that the disciples should teach others; new believers or the people they had influenced—into becoming new believers to guide them in spiritual growth and obedience to the Word. This intention of Christ was to be a continuation of His teaching, with clear communication of the gospel message.

Jesus also promised He would be with them and us always, to the end of the age. He will be with us and protect us as we go. So, the action we all need to initiate is 'going' and allowing Jesus to make us fishers of men. As we go, people will respond, and you will know that you are doing your part in fulfilling the command of the Father.

As you close the pages of this book, remember that eternity hangs in the balance. The souls of men and women are at stake. The Great Commission compels us to step out of our comfort zones, to engage with the lost, and to share the life-transforming message of Jesus. Each encounter is an opportunity to make an eternal impact.

Consider this book your compass. It points you toward lost souls, guiding you to share the hope you have found. In the Soul-Winner's toolbox are the tools that equip you for effective soul-winning. These tools are not physical; they are spiritual. Prayer, the Word of God, empathy, and genuine relationships all contribute to your effectiveness as a soul-winner.

Remember that both heaven and hell await the outcome of your actions. Eternity calls, and you have a role to play. So be effervescent with excitement to share the gospel.

The Soul-winner's Toolbox

PRACTICAL TIPS:

Previously, in chapter two, I discussed the importance of trainers undergoing continuous training to stay updated with changes. Therefore, the trainer must also become a trainee. One of the most valuable resources I received was a booklet titled Your Walk in Christ, which offers lessons for new believers. I would like to share this resource with you in the hope that it may enrich your discipleship program.

The booklet contains six lessons, along with a question segment to support learning. It serves as a guideline for new believers as they begin their walk with Christ.

Your Decision for Christ:

Congratulations on this significant achievement of being made new in Christ! Dear graduate, as you step into this new chapter of your life, remember that God's love and guidance are always with you. May the Lord bless you with wisdom, strength, and peace in all your future endeavours.

You have received Christ as your Saviour, and now as your Saviour: you need to grow in grace and knowledge of the Lord (1 Peter 2:2). These lessons are designed to help you learn how to follow Christ in your Christian life.

The Bible teaches you how to be obedient to Christ. As a new believer, you will need to learn how to study the Bible (the Word of God). You will also need to understand the importance of walking by faith (Hebrews 11:6).

You are blessed as you grow in your knowledge of how to seek God in prayer. You will learn to love the church as you worship and fellowship with God's people. Your heart will be filled with joy as you learn to witness for the Lord Jesus Christ and see others come to know Him as you have.

Be sure to complete the questionnaire at the end of each lesson as you study each section of the booklet. We recommend that you read the scripture references and memorise at least one scripture per week.

The bible says "Thy word have I hid in my heart, that I might not sin against thee" (Psalm 119:11).

Lesson 1

Our First Step In Christ

Trusting Christ and receiving Him as your Saviour is the beginning of your Christian walk. As a believer, Christ now lives in your heart and life (Galatians 2:20). He has come to dwell there so that you might have roots that grow in His love (Ephesians 3:17).

The life that has been given to you is eternal, which means it will last forever (John 3:16; 6:47). God has given you this new life because you believed in Jesus Christ (1 John 5:11-13). You are now under the special care of God, who will bless you as you follow Christ, accepting and believing in His promises (Matthew 6:25-33).

Since you are now a part of God's family, temptation will increase. You are part of the army of God. As a soldier for Christ, you will be engaged in battle. You will need to put on the whole "Armour of the Lord" (Ephesians 6:10-17).

Lesson 2: Confessing Christ

When we confess Christ publicly before others, it confirms our relationship with the Lord (Matthew 10:32).

- To confess means to admit or acknowledge sin; it involves being in agreement with Him. When we confess Jesus, we align our words with His truth. For instance, Jesus declared, "I am the way, the truth, and the life" (John 14:6). To confess Him means saying, "For me, Jesus is my way, truth, and life." It is not merely considering His words; it is about owning them and trusting Him as Lord, Teacher, and Saviour.

- Romans 10:9-13 teaches us that we must believe with our hearts, and with our mouths, confession is made.

- **Speak openly about Jesus:** Share your faith with others. Talk about His love, grace, and salvation.

- **Be honest and kind:** Let your words reflect Christ's character.

- Baptism shows our obedience to Christ and identifies us with a visible church (Acts 16:30-33).

- It symbolises the death, burial, and resurrection of Jesus Christ. It represents the new life we have found in Him (Romans 6:4-6). Jesus set the example when He was baptised by John the Baptist.

- It is very important for new believers to share with others what has happened to them. Your friends and family may not understand, but it is an expectation from God that you confess the truth you have experienced.

QUESTIONS:

1. What does Romans 10.9 teach us?

2. How should you be baptised? (Acts 8.38)

3. Who should be baptised according to?

A. Mark 16;16:

B. Acts 2.41:

C. Acts 18.8:

D. Acts 16.31-33:

ne of God's children, therefore you will need to learn how to act, how to live, and how to walk in God's light (Ephesians 5:1-11).

"That if you confess with your mouth the Lord Jesus and shalt believe in thine heart that god hath raised him from the dead, thou shall be saved,"

Spiritual Armour Explain:
- Put on the "**belt of truth**"- The truth has set you free and will keep you free (John 8:32). You will know the truth, and it will set you free.

- "**Breastplate of Righteousness**"- The breastplate guards our hearts and ensures we stand firm against the schemes of the enemy. Through faith in Jesus, we are made "right" with God, and His righteousness becomes our protective breastplate (2 Corinthians 5:21).

- The **gospel of peace**"- Having "shod your feet with the preparation of the gospel of peace." Our shoes equip us to move swiftly, stand firm, and share the good news. It not only brings personal assurance but also empowers us to impact others with God's love and salvation. We study the Word of God and apply its teachings in our lives (Romans 1:15).

- "**Shield of Faith**" – The shield means actively trusting in God and His Word. As we believe in God's promises, our faith becomes a protective shield, empowering us to stand firm and trust that God's victory will lead us through any challenges (Timothy 6:12).

- Helmet of Salvation"- The spiritual helmet guards our minds and thoughts. As believers, we face spiritual battles, temptations, doubts, and attacks from the enemy (Satan). It reminds us that our victory does not depend on our strength but on God's power. When we wear the **helmet of salvation**, we ward off fear and doubt. Our confidence comes from accepting Jesus as our Lord. We're no longer vulnerable; God protects our minds. It provides assurance that our salvation is secure and that we belong to God (Thessalonians 5:8).

- "**Sword of the Spirit**" The sword equips us to stand firm, declaring God's truth in the face of adversity. It is the Word of God, both written and spoken, that we wield against spiritual enemies. The sword is the offensive weapon we use to defend the gospel (good news) (Hebrews 4:12).

1. Prayer is the power that holds the in place; it is the thread that weaves our spiritual armour together, empowering us to face spiritual battles with confidence.

2. **Practical Application**:
    - When you put on the belt of truth, pray for integrity.
    - With the **breastplate** of righteousness, seek God's righteousness.
    - As you wear the shoes of the gospel of peace, pray for peace and boldness to share the gospel.
    - Faith, salvation, and the Word of God (the sword of the Spirit) are all fortified by prayer.

Memorise: John 10:10 Jesus said "I have come that they might have an abundant life."

Lesson 4: Following Christ in Prayer:

It is very important that you know how to pray. The disciples asked Jesus to teach them how to pray (Luke 11:1).

Prayer is not just a set of words; it is an invitation to commune with God, expressing our hearts and seeking His presence. The Lord encourages us to pray so He can meet our needs.

Through prayer, we receive forgiveness of sins (1 John 1:9). Prayer is essential to the work of God. It provides strength during adversity, reminding us that we're not alone and that there's a greater purpose beyond our immediate circumstances.

Additionally, prayer allows us to express gratitude for our blessings.

Questions:

What does the following scriptures say about prayer?

James 5:16:_____

Matthew 6:6:_____

Romans 8:26:_____

Mark 11:24:_____

Lesson 5: Christ said: search the Scriptures"

Jesus said, "You search the Scriptures," referring to the entire Bible, for it is God's word to us (Psalm 119:105; John 5:39).

The word of God is food for us; we are to grow in grace and knowledge of the Lord. To grow as a follower of Christ, you must study the Scriptures (Matthew 4:4; 2 Peter 3:18).

The only way we can please God is by living in faith (Hebrews 11:6). We receive faith by hearing the word of God (Romans 10:17).

The Bible teaches us how to have victory in our lives (1 John 5:4). The Scriptures serve as a map, pointing to a priceless treasure: salvation in Jesus. They reveal God's love for humanity and His plan to reconcile us to Himself.

Questions:

Explain how the word of God can help you according to :

Psalm 119:11_____

John 8: 31-32_____

Acts 20:32_____

2 Timothy 2:15_____

Psalm 119:165_____

Romans 10:17_____

Lesson 6: Witnessing for Christ:

Jesus said, "You shall be my witnesses." One of God's greatest blessings is allowing you and me to testify for Jesus Christ.

Witnessing simply means telling others what we've personally experienced with the Lord Jesus. For instance, when we received Jesus as our Savior, we might have shared our salvation experience and how wonderful it was with our friends or family.

Witnessing is sharing with others what Jesus has done for you. Being a witness for God involves effectively sharing your faith and spreading the gospel message.

We will be witnesses to the whole world, starting at home and reaching out to all nations (Acts 1:8). It is God's will that everyone should be saved (2 Peter 3:9). Unless you and I share the gospel, most people in the world will never know salvation.

The Lord will help you share the good news of Jesus Christ. We should follow the example of those early believers (John 4:39; Romans 1:8; Acts 4:13; 1 Thessalonians 1:8).

Questions: what does the following scriptures teach about the plan of salvation?

John 3:16 _____

Romans 3:23 _____

Revelations 3:20 _____

Romans 5:8 _____

John 10:10 _____

John 1:10 _____

Memorise: Acts 2:21 "and it shall come to pass, that whosoever shall call on the name of the Lord shall be saved."

Reflection:

1. How will you connect with God this week?

_____

_____

_____

_____

_____

_____

2. Where do you see yourself on the scale of seeking to evangelise your community?

_____

_____

_____

_____

_____

3. How Will You Take Action?

_____
_____
_____
_____
_____
_____

4. What Scriptures inspire and guide your evangelistic conversations?

_____
_____
_____
_____
_____
_____

In the next chapter we will be exploring the essence of church planting the nurturing process, growth, and the establishment of a strong foundation in faith by Planting Seeds of Faith:

CHAPTER SIX:
PLANTING SEEDS OF FAITH

In this chapter, we are privileged to welcome insights from **Pastor Alex Brito**, a seasoned pastor and evangelist with a background in business and theology in Brazil. Pastor Alex has dedicated his life to spreading the Gospel and church planting while training others to do the same. As the city catalyst for the London project and pastor of Mosiac Multicultural church he has led numerous joint church evangelistic outreach, equipping believers with practical tools and strategies to share their faith effectively.

Pastor Alex's expertise and passion for church planting evangelism bring a wealth of knowledge to this chapter. His practical advice and real-life examples will inspire and empower you to embrace the call of church planting through evangelism and reach others with the love of Christ.

The Art of Spiritual Planting

Why should we plant churches? Is there a compelling reason for it, especially in areas where existing churches struggle to grow? Wouldn't it be more impactful to focus only on evangelism instead? Besides, in Matthew 28:19-20, did Jesus instruct the disciples to "go and plant churches"?

Firstly, while evangelism is vital for spreading the gospel, planting new churches is equally essential for creating lasting communities that engage and nurture believers over time. Disciples are formed not only through evangelism but also by a discipleship process within a local church community.

Secondly, the New Testament provides numerous examples showing the vital relationship between evangelism and church planting. For instance, in Acts 2:14-41, we see Peter share the gospel, followed by the formation and growth of a new church in verses 42-47. This illustrates the transformative power of both evangelism and church planting.

Lastly, some experts have observed that new churches are often more effective at reaching non-Christians. This is why prominent missiologists like C. Peter Wagner argue that "planting new churches is the most effective evangelistic methodology known under heaven." Tim Keller also points out, "One church, no matter how large, will never be able to meet the diverse needs of a city."

In summary, evangelism and church planting work together to enhance our capacity to share the gospel with a wider audience. Therefore, we need to engage in church planting. But how do we begin planting new churches? What actions should we take? Let's focus on the seven essential Ps as a guide.

Prayer

Church planting is a challenging endeavour involving a significant aspect of spiritual warfare that should not be underestimated. Francis Schaeffer once stated, "What we are doing is not just difficult; it is impossible." This emphasises that church planting is a supernatural undertaking that cannot be accomplished without God's assistance.

Moreover, starting a church should never be motivated by selfish ambitions, such as expanding a denomination or personal ministry. This temptation is a common struggle for many planters. Instead, churches should be established to advance God's Kingdom and give Him the glory He deserves, a godly ambition.

We must pray to God to avoid temptation and safeguard ourselves from spiritual attacks. Prayer is essential in this process, helping us rely on God effectively.

Planter

Ideally, a church plant needs a church planter, like churches need pastors. It's important to clarify that there is no significant distinction between a church planter and a pastor. While being a gifted entrepreneur, communicator, counsellor, and leader is valuable, these traits alone do not qualify someone as a church planter.

Specific spiritual qualifications are essential for the role of a planet as it is for a pastor. According to the New Testament, there are different lists of qualifications for pastors and church planters, such as those found in 1 Timothy 3:1-7 and Titus 1:5, 7.

These qualifications for church planters do not suggest that they belong to a higher class of Christians. As D.A. Carson explains, "what is required, in some sense, of all believers is especially required of the leaders of believers."[1] In fact, a church planter is just like everyone else, serving as an example for others to follow.

Plan

There are various methods for planting new churches, but three main models are commonly used.

Some church plants focus on revitalising or replanting an existing church that has become inactive or lifeless.

Other churches are planted through a church that identifies, trains, and sends out a team to establish a new congregation in a different location.

Another approach involves creating a new church from scratch through the efforts of an entrepreneurial planter.

There is no perfect model, and each has advantages and disadvantages. The important thing is to decide which model would best suit a location's needs.

People

An essential quality for a church planter is the ability to recruit effectively. This process focuses not on drawing individuals away from other churches, but on connecting with mission-minded people who are enthusiastic about contributing to the work that God has called you to do. By building a dedicated and collaborative team, you can create a thriving church that engages and impacts the community.

---

[1] D. A. Carson, The Cross and Christian Ministry (Grand Rapids: Baker, 1993), 95

On the other hand, having the wrong team will lead to unnecessary conflicts and frustration. Therefore, when recruiting a team, invite individuals to commit wholeheartedly and view themselves as active local missionaries.

It's essential that they aren't just church attendees but rather dedicated team members ready to serve alongside you. Together, we will answer Jesus' call for labourers to enter the harvest with purpose and conviction.

Place

Choosing the right location for planting a church is a vital process that requires careful consideration and thorough research. Besides relying on God for guidance, the planter and the team needs to focus on a series of factors and questions. Is the area spiritually receptive? Does your church have an established social network in the area? Does the leader of the new church possess local knowledge and relationships in the community?

If you can answer "yes" to all of these questions, it indicates that your church and its leaders have a solid grasp of the potential area, which can greatly enhance the likelihood of a successful church plant. If you're unable to respond positively, consider it an opportunity to conduct further research and engage more with the community.

This might also suggest that the location requires deeper examination before moving forward. Embrace this proactive approach to thoroughly assess these factors, ensuring you make a well-informed decision for your church's future.

Pounds

Although financial resources might not be your primary motivation for starting a church, securing funds is essential for ensuring your ministry thrives and expands.

There are numerous effective strategies to raise money for your church plant, and the most suitable approach will depend on your unique network, connections with other churches, denominational affiliations, and local context.

Here are two powerful strategies to secure the necessary funds. One, build strong relationships with your denomination, other churches, and individuals who actively support ministries. Proactively seek their backing to meet the financial needs of your church plant. Two, consider launching a side business or taking on a second job to generate additional income specifically for your church.

This strategy bolsters your funding and allows your business or second job to serve as a vibrant ministry and a platform for church growth.

Partnership

If a church's ultimate goal is to expand God's kingdom and glorify Him, then simply planting individual churches will fall short. The spiritual needs and opportunities within our cities are far too immense for any church to address. We must actively pursue collaboration among churches, denominations, and networks.

By working together, we can significantly enhance our impact in our communities, regardless of their size, and share the message of Jesus with a much larger audience. Besides, since God is the one who saves Christians, and they will spend eternity together, there is no reason for churches not to start collaborating now.

These partnerships operate at three distinct levels. Level 1 involves churches within the same denomination that firmly align on their theological convictions. Level 2, churches that may have minor theological differences yet share a powerful commitment to common causes like evangelism or church planting. Level 3, churches with significant theological differences—such as egalitarianism versus complementarianism—can still unite to tackle urgent needs, prioritising acts of compassion and the mission to reach the lost.

This collaborative spirit showcases the strength of unity in purpose, regardless of doctrinal nuances.

Conclusion

We hope you find Pastor Alex Brito's insights both enlightening and motivating. His dedication to church planting through evangelism his practical approach provide invaluable tools for your own evangelistic efforts.

Chapter summary/Key takeaways:

- The church's ultimate goal is to expand God's kingdom and glorify Him.
- Evangelism and church planting work together to enhance our capacity to share the gospel.
- Location plays a vital part in church planting.
- An essential quality for a church planter is the ability to recruit effectively dedicated and collaborative team.

The Soul-winner's Toolbox

TESTIMONIALS

The purpose of the testimonial page is twofold: first, to encourage individual Christians to get involved in sharing the gospel of Jesus with their friends. Although this task is not always easy, indeed, it is often difficult and can be challenging. I want to emphasize that it is an immensely rewarding privilege that God has given us all through the gospel. Secondly, this page aims to introduce you to the why, when, where, who, and how of practical evangelism that works and achieves results.

Here, I will feature real stories about individuals who have experienced the transformative effects of my evangelism efforts.

1. Title: "From a Park Bench to Eternal Hope"

Introduction: I want to share a remarkable encounter I had at the local park. It was a sunny day, and I decided to take a walk during my fasting session. Little did I know that God had orchestrated a divine appointment.

- As I walked through the park, I noticed a young man walking with his head down, lost in thought. I felt the prompting of the Spirit telling me to go and talk with him. I began walking briskly to catch up, calling out as I got closer. He stopped, and I introduced myself, we exchanged greetings. He invited me to sit on a bench, and I sensed an openness in his heart.
- I asked him about his life, and he explained that he was not a Christian. He asked me how many times a person could accept Jesus as their personal Saviour.

Seeds of Truth:

- I felt prompted to share my own journey of faith. I talked about how Jesus had transformed my life and how His love had rescued me from darkness.

- We discussed the Bible, grace, and forgiveness, including the story of Nicodemus and what it means to be born again. I emphasized that accepting Jesus is a heart matter; He isn't just a historical figure but a living Saviour who longs to know him personally.

The Turning Point:
- His body language changed as I shared the story of the cross using the three-circle method, the ultimate sacrifice for our sins.
- He confessed his need for a Saviour. Right there, on that park bench, he surrendered his life to Christ. We prayed together, and I witnessed the weight of guilt lift from his shoulders.

Joy Overflowing:
- The joy that followed was indescribable. We laughed, shook hands as a point of agreement, and praised God. Suddenly, the sunlight felt warmer. He was happy, I was happy; we asked a passerby to take a picture of us together and exchanged telephone numbers.

- He asked, "What now?" I assured him that he was part of God's family, and that we would walk this journey together. I shared gospel literature (tract) titled "The Gift of Love" along with my church details, and he was pleased for me to contact him and share more about the gift of salvation.

Conclusion: That park bench became an altar, a place of transformation. I left with a renewed sense of purpose, knowing that God had used me to bring someone into His kingdom. Our encounter reminded me that God's love knows no boundaries, and that His grace is available to all.

2. Title: "From Parenting Partnership to Eternal Purpose"

Introduction: As a nursery manager, my days are filled with speaking to parents and ensuring children's welfare and safety. However, one day, God orchestrated a divine appointment that would forever change my perspective.

Before Christ: My client, "Z," is the mother of three children. By the world's standards, she is raising her children correctly, and they seem content. Yet, beneath that exterior, she carried a burden. We discussed child "N's" progress at the nursery, but our conversations often veered into deeper waters—life's purpose, her loss of another child, how this impacted her parenting style, previous relationships, and the ache for something more.

The Turning Point: One morning, "Z" was the first parent at the nursery, and we engaged in a deep spiritual conversation. I listened, sensing God's nudging. The Holy Spirit whispered, "Share the hope you've found."

The Gospel Conversation: I shared my own journey, the emptiness before Christ, the moment I surrendered, and the joy of knowing Him. "Z" leaned in, hungry for answers. I opened the Bible, and read John 3:16: "For God so loved the world…" I also shared Jeremiah 29:11, which speaks of God's plan for her future. Tears welled up in "Z's" eyes. I felt this was a God-appointed moment!

The Prayer of Surrender: In the nursery classroom, "Z" bowed her head. I prayed, inviting Jesus into her heart. She confessed her need for a Saviour, and I could see the weight lift from her. She seemed lighter, and as she smiled, it was as if heaven rejoiced. "Z's" parenting relationship problems mattered less; her eternal security was now assured.

After Christ: What was most remarkable was her return to the nursery a few days later, excitedly telling me how she had started reading her Bible at home and was planning to join her local church. She now understands the need to pray and have a relationship with God.

Conclusion: I realised that my role as a nursery manager was more than just serving parents and children, it was about souls. God has blessed me with the nursery as my community so that it can be a platform to share the gospel with non-believers. My goal is to set them free from the captivity of their mindsets, to share a word of encouragement according to Isaiah 61:1-3. My first and foremost role is pointing the parents to a relationship with God, teaching the children about who Jesus is, and how to pray as a means of investing in their salvation. I'm reminded that leading someone to Christ is the most rewarding transaction of all.

Below I have included a brief pictorial of a variety of evangelism outreach

The Soul-winner's Toolbox

Weekly Saturday morning
evangelism outreach.

Evangelizing during COVID.

Speaking with young men, sharing
the reason for salvation.

Park Expo weekend 2023.

Young man in the park gives his life to Christ in March 2024.

Facilitating evangelism training with Peter from OAC Ministries UK during lockdown.

Conducting evangelism training at DCM Church Jamaica on January 22, 2024, with positive feedback.

Feedback from training I conducted at Disciples Covenant Ministries Church Jamaica January 2024:

- My takeaway is to remember to keep my eyes open when praying during evangelism on the street or when invited into people's homes. —K. B.
- Remember, testimonials are powerful tools for inspiring others and building trust. By sharing authentic stories, you strengthen your evangelism message and encourage more people to join your cause.

3. Practical experience: Testimonial By Rev. Fitzroy. A. Williams

I pastor a small church located in a rural community in the North Eastern area of Jamaica. The community is predominantly a farming area, with a population of about seven thousand people. The area is mostly hilly and very ideal for raising a family, conducting business, and enjoying the cool atmosphere generally presented.

Our church, Disciples Covenant Ministries, conducted a training on evangelism in February 2024, facilitated by Nicole Bennett-Blake. This training was indeed an eye-opener, as she exposed us to the different cultural aspects of spreading the gospel and, most importantly, to the many opportunities available through our daily interactions with people.

For example, we can engage with others at the store, on the bus, going to church, or taking a stroll in the park.

Subsequently, the training has helped participants gain confidence in sharing their faith boldly, introducing others to Christ, approaching anyone at any time, enjoying the experience while evangelizing, and being supported by other members through prayer.

In conclusion, we have benefited immensely from this training. We recommend this training and her books to other churches; the materials provided by Nicole Bennett-Blake are biblically aligned and supported by proven testimonials such as this.

Rev. Fitzroy. A. Williams, *JP - pastor at Disciples Covenant Ministries Jamaica. www.dcmja.org*

CHAPTER SIX

In this chapter, we are privileged to welcome insights from **Pastor Alex Brito**, a seasoned pastor and evangelist with a background in business and theology in Brazil. Pastor Alex has dedicated his life to spreading the Gospel and church planting while training others to do the same. As the city catalyst for the London project and pastor of Mosiac Multicultural church he has led numerous joint church evangelistic outreach, equipping believers with practical tools and strategies to share their faith effectively.

Pastor Alex's expertise and passion for church planting evangelism bring a wealth of knowledge to this chapter. His practical advice and real-life examples will inspire and empower you to embrace the call of church planting through evangelism and reach others with the love of Christ.

Main Content

Why should we plant churches? Is there a compelling reason for it, especially in areas where existing churches struggle to grow? Wouldn't it be more impactful to focus only on evangelism instead? Besides, in Matthew 28:19-20, did Jesus instruct the disciples to "go and plant churches"?

Firstly, while evangelism is vital for spreading the gospel, planting new churches is equally essential for creating lasting communities that engage and nurture believers over time. Disciples are formed not only through evangelism but also by a discipleship process within a local church community.

Secondly, the New Testament provides numerous examples showing the vital relationship between evangelism and church planting. For instance, in Acts 2:14-41, we see Peter share the gospel, followed by the formation and growth of a new church in verses 42-47. This illustrates the transformative power of both evangelism and church planting.

Lastly, some experts have observed that new churches are often more effective at reaching non-Christians. This is why prominent missiologists like C. Peter Wagner argue that "planting new churches is the most effective evangelistic methodology known under heaven." Tim Keller also points out, "One church, no matter how large, will never be able to meet the diverse needs of a city."

In summary, evangelism and church planting work together to enhance our capacity to share the gospel with a wider audience. Therefore, we need to engage in church planting. But how do we begin planting new churches? What actions should we take? Let's focus on the seven essential Ps as a guide.

Prayer

Church planting is a challenging endeavour involving a significant aspect of spiritual warfare that should not be underestimated. Francis Schaeffer once stated, "What we are doing is not just difficult; it is impossible." This emphasises that church planting is a supernatural undertaking that cannot be accomplished without God's assistance.

Moreover, starting a church should never be motivated by selfish ambitions, such as expanding a denomination or personal ministry. This temptation is a common struggle for many planters. Instead, churches should be established to advance God's Kingdom and give Him the glory He deserves, a godly ambition.

We must pray to God to avoid temptation and safeguard ourselves from spiritual attacks. Prayer is essential in this process, helping us rely on God effectively.

Planter

Ideally, a church plant needs a church planter, like churches need pastors. It's important to clarify that there is no significant distinction between a church planter and a pastor. While being a gifted entrepreneur, communicator, counsellor, and leader is valuable, these traits alone do not qualify someone as a church planter.

Specific spiritual qualifications are essential for the role of a planet as it is for a pastor. According to the New Testament, there are different lists of qualifications for pastors and church planters, such as those found in 1 Timothy 3:1-7 and Titus 1:5, 7.

These qualifications for church planters do not suggest that they belong to a higher class of Christians. As D.A. Carson explains, "what is required, in some sense, of all believers is especially required of the leaders of believers."[2] In fact, a church planter is just like everyone else, serving as an example for others to follow.

Plan

There are various methods for planting new churches, but three main models are commonly used.

Some church plants focus on revitalising or replanting an existing church that has become inactive or lifeless.

Other churches are planted through a church that identifies, trains, and sends out a team to establish a new congregation in a different location.

Another approach involves creating a new church from scratch through the efforts of an entrepreneurial planter.

There is no perfect model, and each has advantages and disadvantages. The important thing is to decide which model would best suit a location's needs.

People

An essential quality for a church planter is the ability to recruit effectively. This process focuses not on drawing individuals away from other churches, but on connecting with mission-minded people who are enthusiastic about contributing to the work that God has called you to do. By building a dedicated and collaborative team, you can create a thriving church that engages and impacts the community.

---

[2] D. A. Carson, The Cross and Christian Ministry (Grand Rapids: Baker, 1993), 95

On the other hand, having the wrong team will lead to unnecessary conflicts and frustration. Therefore, when recruiting a team, invite individuals to commit wholeheartedly and view themselves as active local missionaries.

It's essential that they aren't just church attendees but rather dedicated team members ready to serve alongside you. Together, we will answer Jesus' call for labourers to enter the harvest with purpose and conviction.

Place

Choosing the right location for planting a church is a vital process that requires careful consideration and thorough research. Besides relying on God for guidance, the planter and the team needs to focus on a series of factors and questions. Is the area spiritually receptive? Does your church have an established social network in the area? Does the leader of the new church possess local knowledge and relationships in the community?

If you can answer "yes" to all of these questions, it indicates that your church and its leaders have a solid grasp of the potential area, which can greatly enhance the likelihood of a successful church plant. If you're unable to respond positively, consider it an opportunity to conduct further research and engage more with the community.

This might also suggest that the location requires deeper examination before moving forward. Embrace this proactive approach to thoroughly assess these factors, ensuring you make a well-informed decision for your church's future.

Pounds

Although financial resources might not be your primary motivation for starting a church, securing funds is essential for ensuring your ministry thrives and expands.

There are numerous effective strategies to raise money for your church plant, and the most suitable approach will depend on your unique network, connections with other churches, denominational affiliations, and local context.

Here are two powerful strategies to secure the necessary funds. One, build strong relationships with your denomination, other churches, and individuals who actively support ministries. Proactively seek their backing to meet the financial needs of your church plant. Two, consider launching a side business or taking on a second job to generate additional income specifically for your church.

This strategy bolsters your funding and allows your business or second job to serve as a vibrant ministry and a platform for church growth.

Partnership

If a church's ultimate goal is to expand God's kingdom and glorify Him, then simply planting individual churches will fall short. The spiritual needs and opportunities within our cities are far too immense for any church to address. We must actively pursue collaboration among churches, denominations, and networks.

By working together, we can significantly enhance our impact in our communities, regardless of their size, and share the message of Jesus with a much larger audience. Besides, since God is the one who saves Christians, and they will spend eternity together, there is no reason for churches not to start collaborating now.

These partnerships operate at three distinct levels. Level 1 involves churches within the same denomination that firmly align on their theological convictions. Level 2, churches that may have minor theological differences yet share a powerful commitment to common causes like evangelism or church planting. Level 3, churches with significant theological differences—such as egalitarianism versus complementarianism—can still unite to tackle urgent needs, prioritising acts of compassion and the mission to reach the lost.

This collaborative spirit showcases the strength of unity in purpose, regardless of doctrinal nuances.

Conclusion

We hope you find Pastor Alex Brito's insights both enlightening and motivating. His dedication to church planting through evangelism his practical approach provide invaluable tools for your own evangelistic efforts.

Chapter summary/Key takeaways:

- The church's ultimate goal is to expand God's kingdom and glorify Him.
- Evangelism and church planting work together to enhance our capacity to share the gospel.
- Location plays a vital part in church planting.
- An essential quality for a church planter is the ability to recruit effectively dedicated and collaborative team.

CONCLUSION

"Harvest of Hearts: Cultivating Effective Evangelism"

As we close this chapter, let us gather the tools we've sharpened the seeds of grace, the watering cans of compassion, and the sickles of truth. The harvest awaits, and the fields stretch wide.

1. **The Art of Listening**: We've learned that evangelism begins with attentive ears. Listening to others' stories opens doors, builds bridges, and softens hearts. Let us be listeners first, sowing seeds of trust.

2. **The Power of Storytelling**: Our testimonies are not mere narratives; they are living epistles, inked by grace and sealed by redemption. As we share our stories, let us remember that the Hero is Jesus the One who transforms, forgives, and calls us His own.

3. **Nurturing New Life**: Discipling new converts is a sacred privilege. We've explored the stages of salvation, the importance of holiness, and the joy of modelling a vibrant Christian life. May we continue to walk alongside these spiritual infants, feeding them with the milk of God's Word.

4. **Unveiling Grace**: Sharing our faith is not about eloquence; it's about obedience. Whether in everyday conversations or life-altering discussions, let us wield our stories with grace, pointing to the Author of salvation.

As we close this chapter, may our hearts remain tender, our hands open, and our eyes fixed on the fields ripe for harvest.

Nicole Bennett Blake

"Now take the most important step of your Christian journey, reach out to someone today and share the life-changing message of the gospel!"

RECOMMENDED READING RESOURCES:

For further study on evangelism techniques, consider reading the following books:

Soul Winning: How to Share God's Love and Life to a World in Despair" by T.L. Osborn:

- This empowering book equips believers to reach beyond church walls and touch an unconverted world.
- It shares timeless truths, practical methods, and insights used by the Osborn family in their global evangelistic ministry.

"Evangelism Made Simple: 6 Easy Steps" by Nicole Bennett Blake:

This book provides practical strategies for sharing your faith. Here's what you can expect:

1. **Testimony Sharing:**
   - Learn how to share your personal testimony effectively.
   - Gain insights on using your story to connect with others.
2. **Gospel-Centered Approach:**
   - The book draws from the Gospel of John, emphasizing a Christ-centered message.
   - Discover practical tools for street evangelism.

This resource is valuable for those seeking straightforward guidance in soul winning. Soul winning involves both compassion and conviction. These books offer essential guidance for sharing the love of Christ effectively!

BIBLIOGRAPHY

1. **Spurgeon, Charles Haddon.** *The Soul Winner: How to Lead Sinners to the Saviour.* Wm. B. Eerdmans Publishing, 1989.
   - This classic book by England's master preacher provides valuable insights on the meaning and methods of evangelism. Spurgeon emphasizes that winning souls is "the chief business of the Christian minister" and the "most royal employment" of every believer in Jesus Christ[1].

2. **Bowland, Terry A.** *Make Disciples! Reaching the Postmodern World for Christ.* Limited preview, 1999.
   - A resource that explores effective ways to reach the postmodern world with the message of Christ.

3. **Street, R. Alan.** *The Effective Invitation: A Practical Guide for the Pastor.* Limited preview.
   - A practical guide for pastors on delivering effective invitations during evangelistic efforts.

4. **Chapman, John.**" Know and *Tell The Gospel"-2nd Edition. Kingsford ,N S W: Matthias Media Sydney 1998*
- Provides *insight on how to communicate the gospel message clearly and winsomely to both believers and non-believers.*

5. **Bennett Blake, N.** *Evangelism Made simple 6 easy steps : Strategies and Solution to share your story 2021*

6. **Kai's Y and G** *Training for Trainers the Movement that changed the world*

7. **Hill, et al.** *Equipping People for Ministry Pathway Press 2003 Cleveland Tennessee*

https://www.cru.org/communities/hs/resources/how-to-follow-up-new-christians

ACKNOWLEDGEMENTS

I am profoundly grateful to the many individuals who contributed to the creation of this book. Their support, encouragement, and expertise have been invaluable. While I cannot name everyone individually, I want to express my heartfelt appreciation to the following:

1. **My Family**:

    - To my loving husband, Craig Blake, thank you for your unwavering encouragement.

    - To my children, your patience during my writing hours and your innocent questions reminded me of the simplicity of faith, meaningful discussions, and endless cups of tea. Your belief in this project fuelled my determination.

2. **Spiritual Pastors** and **Mentors**

    - Reverend Daniel Barnett, my pastor, your guidance, prayers, and biblical insights shaped the core message of this book. Thank you for pouring into my life. Your mentorship has impacted my evangelistic journey, boosting my confidence and deepening my understanding of God's heart for lost souls.

    - Mentor Reverend Fitzroy Williams, a dear friend and trusted man of God, your deep, meaningful conversations bring clarity and a wealth of knowledge, wisdom, and support. You offer insight and tools that help me navigate this journey.

3. **Church Community**:
    - The members of St. Jude New Testament Church of God, your fervent prayers sustained me. Your testimonies of transformed lives inspired these pages.
    - The evangelism team and the Elephant & Castle joint churches evangelism outreach team, your behind-the-scenes work creates an atmosphere where souls encounter God.

4. **Editing and Publishing Team**:
    - Afreen Rahat, your keen eye and constructive feedback refined my words. Thank you for making them shine.
    - Designer Designpixzel, the cover design captures the essence of evangelism. Your creativity speaks volumes.

5. **Friends and Prayer Partners**:
    - Friend Samantha Toussaint, your late-night brainstorming sessions and pep talks kept me going. I want to recognize your investment in my development as a messenger of hope.
    - Maxine Ivey, your words of encouragement and support are a breath of fresh air that always brings reassurance and rays of sunlight.
    - Friend Elana, who drew the initial illustration of my book, allowing my imagination to come alive.
    - Prayer partners Povi, Maxine, and Sam, your intercession covered this project. Your prayers moved mountains. Thank you all!

6. **Inspiring Authors and Evangelists**:

    - John Chapman, your book Know and Tell The Gospel (new Edition)1998] ignited my passion for soul winning. patiently teach you effective evangelism techniques. That is model on compassion and courage

    - Evangelist's Steve Gurnett of OAC Ministries UK and the rest of your team, your effortless dedication to share the gospel and guide others into doing the same I extend my deepest appreciation.

    - Rev. Audrey Browne of NTCG Northampton, your tireless efforts in the harvest field remind me of the urgency of our mission.

7. **Readers and Supporters**:

    - To every reader who picks up this book, may it equip you to share the Gospel boldly.

    - To those who financially supported this project through crowdfunding or pre-orders, your belief in its impact humbles me.

Remember, this book is not just mine; it belongs to all who labour for the Kingdom. May it inspire soul winners around the world.

In His service, Nicole Bennett Blake

Nicole Bennett Blake

ABOUT THE AUTHOR

In 2021, Nicole embarked on her journey to become an author to share her lifelong passion for winning souls. She is actively involved in her local church as part of the Pastoral Leadership Team and serves as the Director of the Evangelism Department. She has worked in evangelism and outreach for over five years.

Her first published book *Evangelism Made Simple, 6 Easy Steps*, offers strategies and solutions for sharing your story. It supports the church's growth by providing biblical leadership training in the area of evangelism, all while working under the direction of Pastor Daniel Barnett and focusing on the Great Commission.

Nicole is a member of Open-Air Campaigners Ministries and serves as the evangelism coordinator for the Joint Churches Evangelism Outreach in her local area. She supports other churches, both nationally and internationally, by providing evangelism training and resources for the "Great Commission."

Nicole holds two degrees: her first in Social Work (BA Hon) obtained in 2002, and her Early Years Professional Status, awarded in 2011, both from the University of North London. Since 2021, she has been documenting her experiences, learnings, and resolutions, becoming an accomplished author and CEO of Creative Ideas Solutions. She also owns and manages an established children's nursery, where she has worked for over eighteen years, focusing on teaching, building relationships, and facilitating learning.

As a strong advocate for children, she is best known for supporting parents of high-energy children and those experiencing speech and language delays. She is deeply involved in the well-being of children and serves as the chairperson for her local authority's Children, Families, and Young People's Network.

Nicole is recognized for her knowledge, experience, and love for children. She has been a noteworthy leader in her profession and in her managerial role. Her professional interests include her latest book, Stop Saying Yes: *How to Say 'No Without Feeling Guilty*, which includes bonus parenting strategies for success. She has also authored *'The Good Parent' and The Happy Child: A Guide for Parents, Caregivers, and Early Years Consultants.*

Her current projects include her soon-to-be-released book, *The Soul-Winner's Toolbox: A Practical Guide for Effective Evangelism.*

In addition to her writing, Nicole is actively involved with a local charity, helping package and deliver food parcels to the shut-in, single parents, and the homeless in her community.

In her free time, Nicole enjoys spending time with her family, going on holidays, and taking long walks while listening to music as a way to relax and reflect.

Nicole Bennett Blake is married to Craig Blake, and the couple lives in South-East London with their three daughters.

Her books are available on:

- **Website**: www.nicoleblake.com
- **Amazon Author Page**: https://www.amazon.com/stores/Nicole-Bennett-Blake/author/B099P29S3V
- **Systeme:** https://nicoleblake1965.systeme.io/
- **Facebook**: https://m.facebook.com/Creative-Ideas-Solutions
- **Twitter**: https://twitter.com/estelnb55?s=21
- **LinkedIn**: https://uk.linkedin.com/in/nicole-bennett
- **Instagram**: https://instagra2m.com/seeking484?utm

Formatted Lucy 31/10/2024 07:53:00
, Justified, Space Before: 0 pt, After: 4 pt, Line spacing: Multiple 1.15 li

Formatted Lucy 31/10/2024 07:53:00
dy (Times New Roman), 12 pt, Not Bold, Not All caps, Not Expanded by / Condensed by

Formatted Lucy 31/10/2024 07:53:00
dy (Times New Roman), 12 pt, Not Bold, Not All caps, Not Expanded by / Condensed by

Formatted Lucy 31/10/2024 07:53:00
dy (Times New Roman), 12 pt, Not Bold, Not All caps, Not Expanded by / Condensed by

Formatted Lucy 31/10/2024 07:53:00
dy (Times New Roman), 12 pt, Not Bold, Not All caps, Not Expanded by / Condensed by

Formatted Lucy 31/10/2024 07:53:00
dy (Times New Roman), 12 pt, Not Bold, Not All caps, Not Expanded by / Condensed by

Formatted Lucy 31/10/2024 07:53:00
dy (Times New Roman), 12 pt, Not Bold, Not All caps, Not Expanded by / Condensed by

Formatted Lucy 31/10/2024 07:53:00
dy (Times New Roman), 11 pt, Not Bold, Not All caps, Not Expanded by / Condensed by

Formatted Lucy 31/10/2024 07:53:00
dy (Times New Roman), 12 pt, Not Bold, Not All caps, Not Expanded by / Condensed by

] **Formatted** Lucy 31/10/2024 07:53:00
dy (Times New Roman), 12 pt, Not Bold, Not All caps, Not Expanded by / Condensed by

] **Formatted** Lucy 31/10/2024 07:53:00
dy (Times New Roman), 12 pt, Not Bold, Not All caps, Not Expanded by / Condensed by

] **Formatted** Lucy 31/10/2024 07:53:00
dy (Times New Roman), 12 pt, Not Bold, Not Italic, Not All caps, Not Expanded by / Conder

3] **Formatted** Lucy 31/10/2024 07:53:00
raph, Numbered + Level: 1 + Numbering Style: 1, 2, 3, … + Start at: 1 + Alignment: Le
: 0.63 cm + Indent at: 1.27 cm, Pattern: Clear

Page 19: [15] Formatted   Lucy   31/10/2024 07:53:00
Paragraph, Numbered + Level: 1 + Numbering Style: 1, 2, 3, … + Start at: 1 + Alignme
ned at: 0.63 cm + Indent at: 1.27 cm, Pattern: Clear

Page 19: [16] Formatted   Lucy   31/10/2024 07:53:00
Paragraph, Numbered + Level: 1 + Numbering Style: 1, 2, 3, … + Start at: 1 + Alignme
ned at: 0.63 cm + Indent at: 1.27 cm, Pattern: Clear

Page 19: [17] Formatted   Lucy   31/10/2024 07:53:00
Paragraph, Numbered + Level: 1 + Numbering Style: 1, 2, 3, … + Start at: 1 + Alignme
ned at: 0.63 cm + Indent at: 1.27 cm, Pattern: Clear

Page 22: [18] Formatted   Lucy   31/10/2024 07:53:00
Paragraph, Numbered + Level: 1 + Numbering Style: 1, 2, 3, … + Start at: 1 + Alignme
ned at: 0.63 cm + Indent at: 1.27 cm, Pattern: Clear (Background 1)

Page 22: [19] Formatted   Lucy   31/10/2024 07:53:00
Paragraph, Indent: Left: 1.27 cm, Space After: 0 pt, Bulleted + Level: 1 + Aligned at: 1.9 cm
2.54 cm, Pattern: Clear (Background 1)

Page 22: [20] Formatted   Lucy   31/10/2024 07:53:00
Paragraph, Space Before: 0 pt, Numbered + Level: 1 + Numbering Style: 1, 2, 3, … + St
nment: Left + Aligned at: 0.63 cm + Indent at: 1.27 cm, Pattern: Clear (Background 1)

Page 22: [21] Formatted   Lucy   31/10/2024 07:53:00
Paragraph, Indent: Left: 1.27 cm, Bulleted + Level: 1 + Aligned at: 1.9 cm + Indent at:
ern: Clear (Background 1)

Page 22: [22] Formatted   Lucy   31/10/2024 07:53:00
Paragraph, Numbered + Level: 1 + Numbering Style: 1, 2, 3, … + Start at: 1 + Alignme
ned at: 0.63 cm + Indent at: 1.27 cm

Page 22: [23] Formatted   Lucy   31/10/2024 07:53:00
Paragraph, Indent: Left: 1.27 cm, Bulleted + Level: 1 + Aligned at: 1.9 cm + Indent at: 2.

Page 22: [24] Formatted   Lucy   31/10/2024 07:53:00
Paragraph, Numbered + Level: 1 + Numbering Style: 1, 2, 3, … + Start at: 1 + Alignme
ned at: 0.63 cm + Indent at: 1.27 cm

Page 22: [25] Formatted   Lucy   31/10/2024 07:53:00

[7] Formatted Lucy   31/10/2024 07:53:00
raph, Indent: Left: 1.27 cm, Bulleted + Level: 1 + Aligned at: 1.9 cm + Indent at: 2.54 cm

[8] Formatted Lucy   31/10/2024 07:53:00
raph, Indent: Left: 0.63 cm, Bulleted + Level: 1 + Aligned at: 1.27 cm + Indent at: 1.9 cm

[9] Formatted Lucy   31/10/2024 07:53:00
raph, Indent: Left: 0.63 cm, Bulleted + Level: 1 + Aligned at: 1.27 cm + Indent at: 1.9 cm

[0] Formatted Lucy   31/10/2024 07:53:00
raph, Indent: Left: 0.63 cm, Bulleted + Level: 1 + Aligned at: 1.27 cm + Indent at: 1.9 cm

[1] Formatted Lucy   31/10/2024 07:53:00
raph, Indent: Left: 0.63 cm, Bulleted + Level: 1 + Aligned at: 1.27 cm + Indent at: 1.9 cm

[2] Formatted Lucy   31/10/2024 07:53:00
raph, Indent: Left: 0.63 cm, Bulleted + Level: 1 + Aligned at: 1.27 cm + Indent at: 1.9 cm

[3] Deleted   Lucy   31/10/2024 07:53:00

[3] Deleted   Lucy   31/10/2024 07:53:00

[3] Deleted   Lucy   31/10/2024 07:53:00

[4] Formatted Lucy   31/10/2024 07:53:00
es New Roman, 12 pt, Font colour: Auto, English (US)

[5] Formatted Lucy   31/10/2024 07:53:00
pace Before: Auto, After: Auto, Line spacing: single, Outline numbered + Level: 1 + Numbe
, 3, … + Start at: 1 + Alignment: Left + Aligned at: 0.63 cm + Tab after: 1.27 cm + Inden

[6] Formatted Lucy   31/10/2024 07:53:00
es New Roman, 12 pt, Font colour: Auto, English (US)

Page 38: [38] Formatted   Lucy   31/10/2024 07:53:00
Font: Times New Roman, 12 pt, Font colour: Auto, English (US)

Page 38: [39] Formatted   Lucy   31/10/2024 07:53:00
Font: Times New Roman, 12 pt, Font colour: Auto, English (US)

Page 38: [40] Formatted   Lucy   31/10/2024 07:53:00
Font: Times New Roman, 12 pt, Font colour: Auto, English (US)

Page 38: [41] Formatted   Lucy   31/10/2024 07:53:00
Font: Times New Roman, 12 pt, Font colour: Auto, English (US)

Page 38: [42] Formatted   Lucy   31/10/2024 07:53:00
Font: Times New Roman, 12 pt, Font colour: Auto, English (US)

Page 38: [42] Formatted   Lucy   31/10/2024 07:53:00
Font: Times New Roman, 12 pt, Font colour: Auto, English (US)

Page 38: [42] Formatted   Lucy   31/10/2024 07:53:00
Font: Times New Roman, 12 pt, Font colour: Auto, English (US)

Page 38: [43] Formatted   Lucy   31/10/2024 07:53:00
Font: Times New Roman, 12 pt, Font colour: Auto, English (US)

Page 38: [43] Formatted   Lucy   31/10/2024 07:53:00
Font: Times New Roman, 12 pt, Font colour: Auto, English (US)

Page 38: [44] Formatted   Lucy   31/10/2024 07:53:00
Font: Times New Roman, 12 pt, Font colour: Auto, English (US)

Page 38: [44] Formatted   Lucy   31/10/2024 07:53:00
Font: Times New Roman, 12 pt, Font colour: Auto, English (US)

Page 38: [44] Formatted   Lucy   31/10/2024 07:53:00
Font: Times New Roman, 12 pt, Font colour: Auto, English (US)

Page 38: [44] Formatted   Lucy   31/10/2024 07:53:00
Font: Times New Roman, 12 pt, Font colour: Auto, English (US)

Page 38: [44] Formatted   Lucy   31/10/2024 07:53:00

[45] Formatted Lucy 31/10/2024 07:53:00
...es New Roman, 12 pt, Font colour: Auto, English (US)

[45] Formatted Lucy 31/10/2024 07:53:00
...es New Roman, 12 pt, Font colour: Auto, English (US)

[45] Formatted Lucy 31/10/2024 07:53:00
...es New Roman, 12 pt, Font colour: Auto, English (US)

[46] Formatted Lucy 31/10/2024 07:53:00
...es New Roman, 12 pt, Font colour: Auto, English (US)

[47] Formatted Lucy 31/10/2024 07:53:00
...es New Roman, 12 pt, Font colour: Auto, English (US)

[48] Formatted Lucy 31/10/2024 07:53:00
...es New Roman, 12 pt, Font colour: Auto, English (US)

[49] Formatted Lucy 31/10/2024 07:53:00
...es New Roman, 12 pt, Font colour: Auto, English (US)

[50] Formatted Lucy 31/10/2024 07:53:00
...es New Roman, 12 pt, Font colour: Auto, English (US)

[50] Formatted Lucy 31/10/2024 07:53:00
...es New Roman, 12 pt, Font colour: Auto, English (US)

[50] Formatted Lucy 31/10/2024 07:53:00
...es New Roman, 12 pt, Font colour: Auto, English (US)

[50] Formatted Lucy 31/10/2024 07:53:00
...es New Roman, 12 pt, Font colour: Auto, English (US)

[51] Formatted Lucy 31/10/2024 07:53:00
...es New Roman, 12 pt, Font colour: Auto, English (US)

[52] Formatted Lucy 31/10/2024 07:53:00
...es New Roman, 12 pt, Font colour: Auto, English (US)

[53] Formatted Lucy 31/10/2024 07:53:00

51: [54] Formatted   Lucy   31/10/2024 07:53:00
: Font colour: Auto

51: [55] Formatted   Lucy   31/10/2024 07:53:00
: Font colour: Auto

51: [55] Formatted   Lucy   31/10/2024 07:53:00
: Font colour: Auto

51: [55] Formatted   Lucy   31/10/2024 07:53:00
: Font colour: Auto

51: [56] Formatted   Lucy   31/10/2024 07:53:00
: Not Bold, Font colour: Auto

51: [56] Formatted   Lucy   31/10/2024 07:53:00
: Not Bold, Font colour: Auto

51: [56] Formatted   Lucy   31/10/2024 07:53:00
: Not Bold, Font colour: Auto

51: [57] Formatted   Lucy   31/10/2024 07:53:00
: Not Bold, Font colour: Auto

51: [57] Formatted   Lucy   31/10/2024 07:53:00
: Not Bold, Font colour: Auto

51: [57] Formatted   Lucy   31/10/2024 07:53:00
: Not Bold, Font colour: Auto

51: [58] Formatted   Lucy   31/10/2024 07:53:00
colour: Auto

51: [58] Formatted   Lucy   31/10/2024 07:53:00
colour: Auto

51: [58] Formatted   Lucy   31/10/2024 07:53:00
colour: Auto

51: [59] Formatted   Lucy   31/10/2024 07:53:00

| 9] Formatted Lucy 31/10/2024 07:53:00 |
r: Auto

| 9] Formatted Lucy 31/10/2024 07:53:00 |
r: Auto

| 9] Formatted Lucy 31/10/2024 07:53:00 |
r: Auto

| 9] Formatted Lucy 31/10/2024 07:53:00 |
r: Auto

| 9] Formatted Lucy 31/10/2024 07:53:00 |
r: Auto

| 0] Formatted Lucy 31/10/2024 07:53:00 |
r: Auto

| 0] Formatted Lucy 31/10/2024 07:53:00 |
r: Auto

| 0] Formatted Lucy 31/10/2024 07:53:00 |
r: Auto

| 0] Formatted Lucy 31/10/2024 07:53:00 |
r: Auto

| 0] Formatted Lucy 31/10/2024 07:53:00 |
r: Auto

| 1] Formatted Lucy 31/10/2024 07:53:00 |
r: Auto

| 1] Formatted Lucy 31/10/2024 07:53:00 |
r: Auto

| 2] Formatted Lucy 31/10/2024 07:53:00 |
r: Auto

| 2] Formatted Lucy 31/10/2024 07:53:00 |

| e 51: [62] Formatted | Lucy | 31/10/2024 07:53:00 |

t colour: Auto

| e 51: [62] Formatted | Lucy | 31/10/2024 07:53:00 |

t colour: Auto

| e 51: [62] Formatted | Lucy | 31/10/2024 07:53:00 |

t colour: Auto

| e 51: [62] Formatted | Lucy | 31/10/2024 07:53:00 |

t colour: Auto

| e 51: [63] Formatted | Lucy | 31/10/2024 07:53:00 |

t colour: Auto

| e 51: [63] Formatted | Lucy | 31/10/2024 07:53:00 |

t colour: Auto

| e 51: [63] Formatted | Lucy | 31/10/2024 07:53:00 |

t colour: Auto

| e 51: [63] Formatted | Lucy | 31/10/2024 07:53:00 |

t colour: Auto

| e 51: [63] Formatted | Lucy | 31/10/2024 07:53:00 |

t colour: Auto

| e 51: [63] Formatted | Lucy | 31/10/2024 07:53:00 |

t colour: Auto

| e 51: [63] Formatted | Lucy | 31/10/2024 07:53:00 |

t colour: Auto

| e 51: [63] Formatted | Lucy | 31/10/2024 07:53:00 |

t colour: Auto

| e 51: [63] Formatted | Lucy | 31/10/2024 07:53:00 |

t colour: Auto

| e 52: [64] Formatted | Lucy | 31/10/2024 07:53:00 |

[4] **Formatted** Lucy 31/10/2024 07:53:00
r: Auto

[4] **Formatted** Lucy 31/10/2024 07:53:00
r: Auto

[5] **Formatted** Lucy 31/10/2024 07:53:00
r: Auto

[5] **Formatted** Lucy 31/10/2024 07:53:00
r: Auto

[5] **Formatted** Lucy 31/10/2024 07:53:00
r: Auto

[5] **Formatted** Lucy 31/10/2024 07:53:00
r: Auto

[5] **Formatted** Lucy 31/10/2024 07:53:00
r: Auto

[5] **Formatted** Lucy 31/10/2024 07:53:00
r: Auto

[5] **Formatted** Lucy 31/10/2024 07:53:00
r: Auto

[5] **Formatted** Lucy 31/10/2024 07:53:00
r: Auto

[6] **Formatted** Lucy 31/10/2024 07:53:00
r: Auto

[6] **Formatted** Lucy 31/10/2024 07:53:00
r: Auto

[6] **Formatted** Lucy 31/10/2024 07:53:00
r: Auto

[7] **Formatted** Lucy 31/10/2024 07:53:00

Page 52: [67] Formatted	Lucy	31/10/2024 07:53:00
Bold, Font colour: Auto		

Page 52: [67] Formatted	Lucy	31/10/2024 07:53:00
Bold, Font colour: Auto		

Page 52: [67] Formatted	Lucy	31/10/2024 07:53:00
Bold, Font colour: Auto		

Page 52: [67] Formatted	Lucy	31/10/2024 07:53:00
Bold, Font colour: Auto		

Page 52: [67] Formatted	Lucy	31/10/2024 07:53:00
Bold, Font colour: Auto		

Page 52: [67] Formatted	Lucy	31/10/2024 07:53:00
Bold, Font colour: Auto		

Page 52: [67] Formatted	Lucy	31/10/2024 07:53:00
Bold, Font colour: Auto		

Page 52: [67] Formatted	Lucy	31/10/2024 07:53:00
Bold, Font colour: Auto		

Page 52: [67] Formatted	Lucy	31/10/2024 07:53:00
Bold, Font colour: Auto		

Page 52: [67] Formatted	Lucy	31/10/2024 07:53:00
Bold, Font colour: Auto		

Page 52: [68] Formatted	Lucy	31/10/2024 07:53:00
Not Bold		

Page 52: [68] Formatted	Lucy	31/10/2024 07:53:00
Not Bold		

Page 52: [69] Formatted	Lucy	31/10/2024 07:53:00
Not Bold		

Page 52: [69] Formatted	Lucy	31/10/2024 07:53:00

[70] Formatted Lucy   31/10/2024 07:53:00
raph, Outline numbered + Level: 1 + Numbering Style: 1, 2, 3, … + Start at: 1 + Alignment:
at: 0.63 cm + Tab after: 0 cm + Indent at: 1.27 cm

[71] Formatted Lucy   31/10/2024 07:53:00
raph, Bulleted + Level: 1 + Aligned at: 1.27 cm + Indent at: 1.9 cm

[72] Formatted Lucy   31/10/2024 07:53:00
raph, Outline numbered + Level: 1 + Numbering Style: 1, 2, 3, … + Start at: 1 + Alignment:
at: 0.63 cm + Tab after: 0 cm + Indent at: 1.27 cm

[73] Formatted Lucy   31/10/2024 07:53:00
raph, Bulleted + Level: 1 + Aligned at: 1.27 cm + Indent at: 1.9 cm

[74] Formatted Lucy   31/10/2024 07:53:00
raph, Outline numbered + Level: 1 + Numbering Style: 1, 2, 3, … + Start at: 1 + Alignment:
at: 0.63 cm + Tab after: 0 cm + Indent at: 1.27 cm

[75] Formatted Lucy   31/10/2024 07:53:00
raph, Bulleted + Level: 1 + Aligned at: 1.27 cm + Indent at: 1.9 cm

[76] Formatted Lucy   31/10/2024 07:53:00
raph, Outline numbered + Level: 1 + Numbering Style: 1, 2, 3, … + Start at: 1 + Alignment:
at: 0.63 cm + Tab after: 0 cm + Indent at: 1.27 cm

[77] Formatted Lucy   31/10/2024 07:53:00
raph, Bulleted + Level: 1 + Aligned at: 1.27 cm + Indent at: 1.9 cm

[78] Formatted Lucy   31/10/2024 07:53:00
raph, Bulleted + Level: 1 + Aligned at: 1.27 cm + Indent at: 1.9 cm

[79] Formatted Lucy   31/10/2024 07:53:00

[79] Formatted Lucy   31/10/2024 07:53:00

[79] Formatted Lucy   31/10/2024 07:53:00

80: [80] Formatted Lucy 31/10/2024 07:53:00

80: [80] Formatted Lucy 31/10/2024 07:53:00

80: [80] Formatted Lucy 31/10/2024 07:53:00

80: [80] Formatted Lucy 31/10/2024 07:53:00

80: [81] Formatted Lucy 31/10/2024 07:53:00

80: [81] Formatted Lucy 31/10/2024 07:53:00

80: [81] Formatted Lucy 31/10/2024 07:53:00

80: [81] Formatted Lucy 31/10/2024 07:53:00

80: [81] Formatted Lucy 31/10/2024 07:53:00

80: [81] Formatted Lucy 31/10/2024 07:53:00

80: [81] Formatted Lucy 31/10/2024 07:53:00

80: [81] Formatted Lucy 31/10/2024 07:53:00

80: [82] Formatted Lucy 31/10/2024 07:53:00
: Not Bold

80: [82] Formatted Lucy 31/10/2024 07:53:00

[2] Formatted	Lucy	31/10/2024 07:53:00

Bold

[2] Formatted	Lucy	31/10/2024 07:53:00

Bold

[3] Formatted	Lucy	31/10/2024 07:53:00

Bold

[3] Formatted	Lucy	31/10/2024 07:53:00

Bold

[3] Formatted	Lucy	31/10/2024 07:53:00

Bold

[3] Formatted	Lucy	31/10/2024 07:53:00

Bold

[3] Formatted	Lucy	31/10/2024 07:53:00

Bold

[3] Formatted	Lucy	31/10/2024 07:53:00

Bold

[3] Formatted	Lucy	31/10/2024 07:53:00

Bold

[3] Formatted	Lucy	31/10/2024 07:53:00

Bold

[3] Formatted	Lucy	31/10/2024 07:53:00

Bold

[4] Formatted	Lucy	31/10/2024 07:53:00

ragraph Font, Font: 11 pt, Font colour: Text 1, Pattern: Clear

[5] Formatted	Lucy	31/10/2024 07:53:00

ragraph Font, Font: 11 pt, Font colour: Text 1, Pattern: Clear

[6] Formatted	Lucy	31/10/2024 07:53:00

Page 86: [87] Formatted   Lucy   31/10/2024 07:53:00
Default Paragraph Font, Font: 11 pt, Font colour: Text 1, Pattern: Clear

Page 86: [87] Formatted   Lucy   31/10/2024 07:53:00
Default Paragraph Font, Font: 11 pt, Font colour: Text 1, Pattern: Clear

Page 86: [87] Formatted   Lucy   31/10/2024 07:53:00
Default Paragraph Font, Font: 11 pt, Font colour: Text 1, Pattern: Clear

Page 86: [87] Formatted   Lucy   31/10/2024 07:53:00
Default Paragraph Font, Font: 11 pt, Font colour: Text 1, Pattern: Clear

Page 86: [87] Formatted   Lucy   31/10/2024 07:53:00
Default Paragraph Font, Font: 11 pt, Font colour: Text 1, Pattern: Clear

Page 86: [87] Formatted   Lucy   31/10/2024 07:53:00
Default Paragraph Font, Font: 11 pt, Font colour: Text 1, Pattern: Clear

Page 86: [88] Formatted   Lucy   31/10/2024 07:53:00
Default Paragraph Font, Font: 11 pt, Font colour: Text 1, Pattern: Clear

Page 86: [88] Formatted   Lucy   31/10/2024 07:53:00
Default Paragraph Font, Font: 11 pt, Font colour: Text 1, Pattern: Clear

Page 86: [88] Formatted   Lucy   31/10/2024 07:53:00
Default Paragraph Font, Font: 11 pt, Font colour: Text 1, Pattern: Clear

Page 86: [88] Formatted   Lucy   31/10/2024 07:53:00
Default Paragraph Font, Font: 11 pt, Font colour: Text 1, Pattern: Clear

Page 86: [88] Formatted   Lucy   31/10/2024 07:53:00
Default Paragraph Font, Font: 11 pt, Font colour: Text 1, Pattern: Clear

Page 86: [88] Formatted   Lucy   31/10/2024 07:53:00
Default Paragraph Font, Font: 11 pt, Font colour: Text 1, Pattern: Clear

Page 86: [88] Formatted   Lucy   31/10/2024 07:53:00
Default Paragraph Font, Font: 11 pt, Font colour: Text 1, Pattern: Clear

Page 86: [88] Formatted   Lucy   31/10/2024 07:53:00

[8] Formatted Lucy   31/10/2024 07:53:00
ragraph Font, Font: 11 pt, Font colour: Text 1, Pattern: Clear

[8] Formatted Lucy   31/10/2024 07:53:00
ragraph Font, Font: 11 pt, Font colour: Text 1, Pattern: Clear

[8] Formatted Lucy   31/10/2024 07:53:00
ragraph Font, Font: 11 pt, Font colour: Text 1, Pattern: Clear

[8] Formatted Lucy   31/10/2024 07:53:00
ragraph Font, Font: 11 pt, Font colour: Text 1, Pattern: Clear

[9] Formatted Lucy   31/10/2024 07:53:00
ragraph Font, Font: 11 pt, Font colour: Text 1, Pattern: Clear

[9] Formatted Lucy   31/10/2024 07:53:00
ragraph Font, Font: 11 pt, Font colour: Text 1, Pattern: Clear

[9] Formatted Lucy   31/10/2024 07:53:00
ragraph Font, Font: 11 pt, Font colour: Text 1, Pattern: Clear

[9] Formatted Lucy   31/10/2024 07:53:00
ragraph Font, Font: 11 pt, Font colour: Text 1, Pattern: Clear

[9] Formatted Lucy   31/10/2024 07:53:00
ragraph Font, Font: 11 pt, Font colour: Text 1, Pattern: Clear

[9] Formatted Lucy   31/10/2024 07:53:00
ragraph Font, Font: 11 pt, Font colour: Text 1, Pattern: Clear

[0] Formatted Lucy   31/10/2024 07:53:00
ragraph Font, Font: 11 pt, Font colour: Text 1, Pattern: Clear

[0] Formatted Lucy   31/10/2024 07:53:00
ragraph Font, Font: 11 pt, Font colour: Text 1, Pattern: Clear

[0] Formatted Lucy   31/10/2024 07:53:00
ragraph Font, Font: 11 pt, Font colour: Text 1, Pattern: Clear

[0] Formatted Lucy   31/10/2024 07:53:00

e 86: [90] Formatted   Lucy   31/10/2024 07:53:00
ult Paragraph Font, Font: 11 pt, Font colour: Text 1, Pattern: Clear

e 86: [90] Formatted   Lucy   31/10/2024 07:53:00
ult Paragraph Font, Font: 11 pt, Font colour: Text 1, Pattern: Clear

e 86: [90] Formatted   Lucy   31/10/2024 07:53:00
ult Paragraph Font, Font: 11 pt, Font colour: Text 1, Pattern: Clear

e 86: [90] Formatted   Lucy   31/10/2024 07:53:00
ult Paragraph Font, Font: 11 pt, Font colour: Text 1, Pattern: Clear

e 86: [90] Formatted   Lucy   31/10/2024 07:53:00
ult Paragraph Font, Font: 11 pt, Font colour: Text 1, Pattern: Clear

e 91: [91] Formatted   Lucy   31/10/2024 07:53:00
: Bold, Font colour: Text 1

e 91: [92] Formatted   Lucy   31/10/2024 07:53:00
 colour: Text 1

e 91: [93] Formatted   Lucy   31/10/2024 07:53:00
 colour: Text 1

e 91: [94] Formatted   Lucy   31/10/2024 07:53:00
 colour: Text 1

e 91: [95] Formatted   Lucy   31/10/2024 07:53:00
: 12 pt

e 91: [96] Formatted   Lucy   31/10/2024 07:53:00
: 12 pt

e 91: [97] Formatted   Lucy   31/10/2024 07:53:00
: 12 pt

e 91: [98] Formatted   Lucy   31/10/2024 07:53:00
: 12 pt

e 91: [99] Formatted   Lucy   31/10/2024 07:53:00

| [101] Formatted | Lucy | 31/10/2024 07:53:00 |

ot

| [102] Formatted | Lucy | 31/10/2024 07:53:00 |

ot

| [103] Formatted | Lucy | 31/10/2024 07:53:00 |

ot

| [104] Formatted | Lucy | 31/10/2024 07:53:00 |

ot

| [105] Formatted | Lucy | 31/10/2024 07:53:00 |

ot

| [106] Formatted | Lucy | 31/10/2024 07:53:00 |

ot, Font colour: Text 1

| [107] Formatted | Lucy | 31/10/2024 07:53:00 |

ot

| [108] Formatted | Lucy | 31/10/2024 07:53:00 |

ot

| [109] Formatted | Lucy | 31/10/2024 07:53:00 |

ot

| [110] Formatted | Lucy | 31/10/2024 07:53:00 |

ot

| [111] Formatted | Lucy | 31/10/2024 07:53:00 |

ot

| [112] Formatted | Lucy | 31/10/2024 07:53:00 |

ot, Font colour: Text 1

| [113] Formatted | Lucy | 31/10/2024 07:53:00 |

ot

| [114] Formatted | Lucy | 31/10/2024 07:53:00 |

| 91: [116] Formatted | Lucy | 31/10/2024 07:53:00 |

: 12 pt

| 91: [117] Formatted | Lucy | 31/10/2024 07:53:00 |

: 12 pt, Font colour: Text 1

| 91: [118] Formatted | Lucy | 31/10/2024 07:53:00 |

: 12 pt

| 91: [119] Formatted | Lucy | 31/10/2024 07:53:00 |

: 12 pt

| 91: [120] Formatted | Lucy | 31/10/2024 07:53:00 |

: 12 pt

| 91: [121] Formatted | Lucy | 31/10/2024 07:53:00 |

: 12 pt

| 91: [122] Formatted | Lucy | 31/10/2024 07:53:00 |

: 12 pt

| 91: [123] Formatted | Lucy | 31/10/2024 07:53:00 |

colour: Text 1

| 91: [124] Formatted | Lucy | 31/10/2024 07:53:00 |

: Bold

| 91: [125] Formatted | Lucy | 31/10/2024 07:53:00 |

: Bold, Font colour: Text 1

| 120: [126] Formatted | Lucy | 31/10/2024 07:53:00 |

: Not Bold

| 120: [127] Formatted | Lucy | 31/10/2024 07:53:00 |

e Before: 12 pt, Numbered + Level: 1 + Numbering Style: 1, 2, 3, … + Start at: 1 + Alignm
igned at: 0.63 cm + Indent at: 1.27 cm

| 120: [128] Formatted | Lucy | 31/10/2024 07:53:00 |

colour: Text 1

ore: 12 pt, Outline numbered + Level: 1 + Numbering Style: 1, 2, 3, … + Start at: 1 + Alignm
gned at: 0.63 cm + Tab after: 1.27 cm + Indent at: 1.27 cm

131] Formatted   **Lucy**   **31/10/2024 07:53:00**

Bold

132] Formatted   **Lucy**   **31/10/2024 07:53:00**

r: Text 1

133] Formatted   **Lucy**   **31/10/2024 07:53:00**

Bold

134] Formatted   **Lucy**   **31/10/2024 07:53:00**

Bold

135] Formatted   **Lucy**   **31/10/2024 07:53:00**

r: Text 1

136] Formatted   **Lucy**   **31/10/2024 07:53:00**

ore: 12 pt, Outline numbered + Level: 1 + Numbering Style: Bullet + Aligned at: 1.27 cm +
cm + Indent at: 1.9 cm

137] Formatted   **Lucy**   **31/10/2024 07:53:00**

138] Formatted   **Lucy**   **31/10/2024 07:53:00**

Bold

139] Formatted   **Lucy**   **31/10/2024 07:53:00**

r: Text 1

140] Formatted   **Lucy**   **31/10/2024 07:53:00**

aph, Outline numbered + Level: 1 + Numbering Style: Bullet + Aligned at: 1.27 cm + Tab a
ndent at: 1.9 cm

141] Formatted   **Lucy**   **31/10/2024 07:53:00**

142] Formatted   **Lucy**   **31/10/2024 07:53:00**

r: Text 1

t: Bold

e 120: [145] Formatted	Lucy	31/10/2024 07:53:00	

t colour: Text 1

e 120: [146] Formatted	Lucy	31/10/2024 07:53:00	

t: Bold

e 120: [147] Formatted	Lucy	31/10/2024 07:53:00	

t colour: Text 1

e 120: [148] Formatted	Lucy	31/10/2024 07:53:00	

mal, Space Before: 12 pt, No bullets or numbering, Pattern: Clear

e 120: [149] Formatted	Lucy	31/10/2024 07:53:00	

t colour: Text 1

e 120: [150] Formatted	Lucy	31/10/2024 07:53:00	

t: Bold

e 120: [151] Formatted	Lucy	31/10/2024 07:53:00	

t colour: Text 1

e 120: [152] Formatted	Lucy	31/10/2024 07:53:00	

t: Bold

e 120: [153] Formatted	Lucy	31/10/2024 07:53:00	

t colour: Text 1

e 120: [154] Formatted	Lucy	31/10/2024 07:53:00	

t: Bold, Font colour: Text 1

e 120: [155] Formatted	Lucy	31/10/2024 07:53:00	

t colour: Text 1

e 121: [156] Formatted	Lucy	31/10/2024 07:53:00	

t: Bold

e 121: [157] Formatted	Lucy	31/10/2024 07:53:00	

t colour: Text 1

| [159] Formatted | Lucy | 31/10/2024 07:53:00 |

Bold

| [160] Formatted | Lucy | 31/10/2024 07:53:00 |

ır: Text 1

| [161] Formatted | Lucy | 31/10/2024 07:53:00 |

Bold

| [162] Formatted | Lucy | 31/10/2024 07:53:00 |

raph, Indent: Left: 1.27 cm, Bulleted + Level: 1 + Aligned at: 3.16 cm + Indent at: 3.8 cm

| [163] Formatted | Lucy | 31/10/2024 07:53:00 |

ır: Text 1

| [164] Formatted | Lucy | 31/10/2024 07:53:00 |

Bold

| [165] Formatted | Lucy | 31/10/2024 07:53:00 |

ır: Text 1

| [166] Formatted | Lucy | 31/10/2024 07:53:00 |

Bold

| [167] Formatted | Lucy | 31/10/2024 07:53:00 |

ft: 1.9 cm, Outline numbered + Level: 4 + Numbering Style: Bullet + Aligned at: 4.44 cm + 3 cm + Indent at: 5.08 cm

| [168] Formatted | Lucy | 31/10/2024 07:53:00 |

ır: Text 1

| [169] Formatted | Lucy | 31/10/2024 07:53:00 |

Bold

| [170] Formatted | Lucy | 31/10/2024 07:53:00 |

ır: Text 1

| [171] Formatted | Lucy | 31/10/2024 07:53:00 |

Bold

colour: Text 1

| 121: [174] Formatted | Lucy | 31/10/2024 07:53:00 |

Paragraph, Indent: Left: 1.27 cm, Bulleted + Level: 1 + Aligned at: 3.17 cm + Indent at: 3

| 121: [175] Formatted | Lucy | 31/10/2024 07:53:00 |

colour: Text 1

| 121: [176] Formatted | Lucy | 31/10/2024 07:53:00 |

colour: Text 1

| 121: [177] Formatted | Lucy | 31/10/2024 07:53:00 |

colour: Text 1

| 121: [178] Formatted | Lucy | 31/10/2024 07:53:00 |

: Not Bold

| 121: [179] Formatted | Lucy | 31/10/2024 07:53:00 |

nt: Left: 0.63 cm, Hanging: 0.63 cm

| 121: [180] Formatted | Lucy | 31/10/2024 07:53:00 |

colour: Text 1

| 121: [181] Formatted | Lucy | 31/10/2024 07:53:00 |

nt: Left: 1.27 cm, Outline numbered + Level: 3 + Numbering Style: Bullet + Aligned at:
after: 3.81 cm + Indent at: 3.81 cm

| 121: [182] Formatted | Lucy | 31/10/2024 07:53:00 |

colour: Text 1

| 124: [183] Formatted | Lucy | 31/10/2024 07:53:00 |

: +Body (Times New Roman), Font colour: Text 1

| 124: [184] Formatted | Lucy | 31/10/2024 07:53:00 |

: +Body (Times New Roman), Font colour: Text 1

| 124: [185] Formatted | Lucy | 31/10/2024 07:53:00 |

Paragraph, Bulleted + Level: 1 + Aligned at: 0.63 cm + Indent at: 1.27 cm

| 124: [186] Formatted | Lucy | 31/10/2024 07:53:00 |

| [188] Formatted | Lucy | 31/10/2024 07:53:00 |

ody (Times New Roman), Font colour: Text 1

| [189] Formatted | Lucy | 31/10/2024 07:53:00 |

aragraph Font, Font: 11 pt, Font colour: Auto

| [190] Formatted | Lucy | 31/10/2024 07:53:00 |

| [191] Formatted | Lucy | 31/10/2024 07:53:00 |

aragraph Font, Font: 11 pt, Font colour: Auto

| [192] Formatted | Lucy | 31/10/2024 07:53:00 |

aragraph Font, Font: 11 pt, Font colour: Auto

| [193] Formatted | Lucy | 31/10/2024 07:53:00 |

aragraph Font, Font: +Body (Times New Roman), 11 pt, Font colour: Auto

| [194] Formatted | Lucy | 31/10/2024 07:53:00 |

ndent: Left: 0 cm

| [195] Formatted | Lucy | 31/10/2024 07:53:00 |

aragraph Font, Font: 11 pt, Font colour: Auto

| [196] Formatted | Lucy | 31/10/2024 07:53:00 |

aragraph Font, Font: 11 pt, Font colour: Auto

| [197] Formatted | Lucy | 31/10/2024 07:53:00 |

aragraph Font, Font: 11 pt, Font colour: Auto

| [198] Formatted | Lucy | 31/10/2024 07:53:00 |

aragraph Font, Font: 11 pt, Font colour: Auto

| [199] Formatted | Lucy | 31/10/2024 07:53:00 |

aragraph Font, Font: 11 pt, Font colour: Auto

| [200] Formatted | Lucy | 31/10/2024 07:53:00 |

aragraph Font, Font: 11 pt, Font colour: Auto

| [201] Formatted | Lucy | 31/10/2024 07:53:00 |

125: [203] Formatted Lucy 31/10/2024 07:53:00
ult Paragraph Font, Font: 11 pt, Font colour: Auto

125: [204] Formatted Lucy 31/10/2024 07:53:00
ult Paragraph Font, Font: 11 pt, Font colour: Auto

125: [205] Formatted Lucy 31/10/2024 07:53:00
ult Paragraph Font, Font: 11 pt, Font colour: Auto

125: [206] Formatted Lucy 31/10/2024 07:53:00
ult Paragraph Font, Font: 11 pt, Font colour: Auto

125: [207] Formatted Lucy 31/10/2024 07:53:00
ult Paragraph Font, Font: 11 pt, Font colour: Auto

125: [208] Formatted Lucy 31/10/2024 07:53:00
ult Paragraph Font, Font: 11 pt, Font colour: Auto

125: [209] Formatted Lucy 31/10/2024 07:53:00
ult Paragraph Font, Font: 11 pt, Font colour: Auto

125: [210] Formatted Lucy 31/10/2024 07:53:00
ult Paragraph Font, Font: 11 pt, Font colour: Auto

125: [211] Formatted Lucy 31/10/2024 07:53:00
ult Paragraph Font, Font: 11 pt, Font colour: Auto

125: [212] Formatted Lucy 31/10/2024 07:53:00
ult Paragraph Font, Font: 11 pt, Font colour: Auto

125: [213] Formatted Lucy 31/10/2024 07:53:00
ult Paragraph Font, Font: 11 pt, Font colour: Auto

125: [214] Formatted Lucy 31/10/2024 07:53:00
: Not Bold, Font colour: Text 1

140: [215] Formatted Lucy 31/10/2024 07:53:00
colour: Black

140: [215] Formatted Lucy 31/10/2024 07:53:00

[215] Formatted	Lucy	31/10/2024 07:53:00
r: Black

[215] Formatted	Lucy	31/10/2024 07:53:00
r: Black

[215] Formatted	Lucy	31/10/2024 07:53:00
r: Black

[215] Formatted	Lucy	31/10/2024 07:53:00
r: Black

[215] Formatted	Lucy	31/10/2024 07:53:00
r: Black

[215] Formatted	Lucy	31/10/2024 07:53:00
r: Black

[216] Formatted	Lucy	31/10/2024 07:53:00
r: Black

[216] Formatted	Lucy	31/10/2024 07:53:00
r: Black

[216] Formatted	Lucy	31/10/2024 07:53:00
r: Black

[216] Formatted	Lucy	31/10/2024 07:53:00
r: Black

[216] Formatted	Lucy	31/10/2024 07:53:00
r: Black

[216] Formatted	Lucy	31/10/2024 07:53:00
r: Black

[216] Formatted	Lucy	31/10/2024 07:53:00
r: Black

[217] Formatted	Lucy	31/10/2024 07:53:00

e 140: [217] Formatted t colour: Black	Lucy	31/10/2024 07:53:00	
e 140: [217] Formatted t colour: Black	Lucy	31/10/2024 07:53:00	
e 140: [217] Formatted t colour: Black	Lucy	31/10/2024 07:53:00	
e 140: [217] Formatted t colour: Black	Lucy	31/10/2024 07:53:00	
e 140: [217] Formatted t colour: Black	Lucy	31/10/2024 07:53:00	
e 140: [217] Formatted t colour: Black	Lucy	31/10/2024 07:53:00	
e 140: [218] Formatted t colour: Black	Lucy	31/10/2024 07:53:00	
e 140: [218] Formatted t colour: Black	Lucy	31/10/2024 07:53:00	
e 140: [219] Formatted t colour: Black	Lucy	31/10/2024 07:53:00	
e 140: [219] Formatted t colour: Black	Lucy	31/10/2024 07:53:00	
e 140: [219] Formatted t colour: Black	Lucy	31/10/2024 07:53:00	
e 140: [219] Formatted t colour: Black	Lucy	31/10/2024 07:53:00